MW00810802

LEARN ITALIAN WITH SHORT STORIES

ISBN: 978-1-987949-87-2

This book is published by Bermuda Word. It has been created with specialized software that produces a three line interlinear format.

Please contact us if you would like a pdf version of this book with different font, font size, or font colors and/or less words per page!

LEARN-TO-READ-FOREIGN-LANGUAGES.COM

Dear Reader and Language Learner!

You're reading the Paperback edition of Bermuda Word's interlinear and pop-up HypLern Reader App. Before you start reading Italian, please read this explanation of our method.

Since we want you to read Italian and to learn Italian, our method consists primarily of word-for-word literal translations, but we add idiomatic English if this helps understanding the sentence.

For example:
Fui   a   un tratto arrestato
Was at a   stroke stopped
[Suddenly I was stopped]

The HypLern method entails that you re-read the text until you know the high frequency words just by reading, and then mark and learn the low frequency words in your reader or practice them with our brilliant App.

Don't forget to take a look at the e-book App with integrated learning software that we offer at learn-to-read-foreign-languages.com! For more info check the last two pages of this e-book!

Thanks for your patience and enjoy the story and learning Italian!

Kees van den End

LEARN-TO-READ-FOREIGN-LANGUAGES.COM

INDICE
INDEX

4 Un Regalo alla Sposa

UN REGALO ALLA SPOSA
A GIFT TO THE BRIDE

Gaspare Carpigna aveva fatto i suoi molti denari in
Gaspar Carpigna had made the his much money in
() (abundance of)

ogni maniera, coll'industria, coll'usura, coll'inganno. Ma
each manner with the hard work with the usury with the deceit But
(with hard work) (with usury) (with deceit)

una volta fatti non vi era uomo più galantuomo di lui
one time done do not there was (a) man more gentleman of him
(once) (than)

e ben disposto a godere onestamente dei beni di
and well placed to enjoy honestly of the goods of
(decided)

questa vita. Invecchiando si era dato anche alla pietà,
this life Aging himself was given too the pity

e faceva recitare molte messe da morto, invitando il
and let recite many masses of (the) dead inviting the
(for)

prete a far colazione nella sua bella casa di
priest to do breakfast in the his beautiful house of
(have) (in)

Macagno, dove aveva giurato di passare i suoi ultimi
Macagno where (he) had sworn of spend the his last
(to) ()

giorni in santa pace.
days in saintly peace

6 Un Regalo alla Sposa

Stava per maritare anche la figliuola a un ricco
Stood for marry off also the daughter to a rich
[He was about to] (his)

possidente di Novara, un bel partito per la figlia d'un
landowner of Novara a nice party for the daughter of a
(catch)

carbonaio all'ingrosso.
charcoal wholesale
(company)

E siccome il cuore di Gaspare Carpigna non era
And since the heart of Gaspar Carpigna not was

chiuso ai soavi affetti della famiglia, e per la sua
closed to the sweet affections of the family and for the his
()

Isolina egli sentiva una tenerezza singolare, così si può
Isolina he felt a tenderness singular so one can
(particular)

pensare se a quel matrimonio egli si preparasse con
think oneself to that marriage he himself prepared with

allegria, con compiacenza, con un fervore insolito che
cheer with complacency with a fervor unusual which

lo ringiovaniva.
him made younger

7 Un Regalo alla Sposa

Già i preparativi erano fatti, fatte le pubblicazioni.
Already the preparations were made done the publications

Lo sposo aveva già regalato un bello astuccio di
The groom had already presented one beautiful (jewel)case of

brillanti e le parenti lontane chi un vaso di cristallo,
diamonds and the relatives distant this one a vase of crystal

chi un ventaglio di madreperla, chi un braccialetto, ecc.
that one a fan of mother of pearl this one a bracelet etc

Isolina, assistita da una sua zia materna, poichè la
Isolina assisted by an her aunt maternal since the
[an aunt of hers]

mamma era morta da un pezzo, attendeva il gran
mother was dead since a piece (she) awaited the great
(while)

giorno con estasi.
day with ecstasy

8 Un Regalo alla Sposa

Lo sposo era bello, ricco, simpatico.
The groom was beautiful rich sympathetic

La vecchia casa detta del Zoccolino, che il Carpigna
The old house told of the Zoccolino that the Carpigna
(told about) ()

aveva acquistata per il fallimento d'un suo socio,
had purchased at the bankruptcy of a his partner
[of a partner of his]

rimessa a nuovo e rinfrescata in tutte le parti, non
rebuild to new and refreshed in all the parts not
[no more

pareva più quel lurido filatoio di una volta, dove il
seemed more that filthy spinning workshop of one time where the
looked like]

povero Battistino Dell'Oro, fallito, rovinato, rosicchiato dai
poor Battistino Dell'Oro failed ruined gnawed from

debiti, si era impiccato per la disperazione a un
debts himself was hanged because of the despair on a
(had)

gancio del portone.
hook of the door

9 Un Regalo alla Sposa

Si diceva sommessamente che il Carpigna avesse
They said softly that the Carpigna had
()

aiutato una mano a rovinarlo e che la messa ch'egli
helped (with) a hand to ruin him and that the mass that he

faceva dire ogni 23 di settembre avesse lo scopo di
made say each 23rd of September had the purpose of

versare un secchio d'acqua sopra una pover'anima del
pour one bucket of water over a poor soul of
(in) the

purgatorio, se c'era bisogno.
purgatory if there was need

Ma eran cose vecchie di trent'anni fa, forse anche di
But were things old of thirty years ago maybe too of

più.
more

Scomparso il filatoio, al suo posto sorse una bella
Disappeared the spinning workshop of the its place arose a beautiful
(from)

casa bianca col portone di cotto, colle persiane verdi,
house white with the door of baked clay with the shutters green
(door frame)

col giardino degradante a scalinate verso il lago, il
with the garden sloping by stairs towards the lake the
(terraces)

Zoccolino insomma, come può vedere ancora chi naviga
Zoccolino in short such as can see yet who navigates
(even) (whoever)

verso Macagno sul lago Maggiore.
towards Macagno on the lake Maggiore

Il giardiniere aveva addobbato il giardino a bandiere e
The gardener had decorated the garden with flags and

a palloncini cinesi, e la notte prima del sacramento fu
with balloons Chinese and the night before of the sacrament was

un continuo sparo di mortaretti e un gran suonare di
a continuous shooting of firecrackers and a large play of

chitarre nelle barche illuminate.
guitars in the boats illuminated

11 Un Regalo alla Sposa

Quelli   dell'altra   riva   del   lago,   vedendo   quei   fuochi,
Those   from the other   shore   of   the lake   seeing   those   fires

dimandavano:
asked
(dimandare; archaic form of domandare)

"Che   cosa   c'è   al   Zoccolino?"
What   thing   there is at the   (Villa) Zoccolino

"È   il   Carpigna   che   marita   la   figliuola."
Is   the   Carpigna   that   marries   the   daughter
(It's)   ()   (to someone else)

"Sposerà   qualche   altro   ladro   usuraio."
(She) Marries   some   other   thief   usurer

"Quando   uno   è   ricco,   c'è   sempre   chi   dice   che   ha
When   one   is   rich   there is   always   (those) who say   that   (he) has

rubato."
stolen
(stolen it)

12 Un Regalo alla Sposa

"Volete sentirla, voi che parlate così?"
Do you want to hear it you that spoke like that

Questi discorsi erano fatti da un gruppo di pescatori,
These talks were done by a group of fishermen

che stavano fumando la pipa innanzi all'osteria di
that were smoking the pipe before at the tavern of
(of the tavern)

Cannero, sull'altra riva.
Cannero on the other shore

C'era dunque il lago di mezzo e tanto largo che vi
There was therefore the lake of (the) middle and so wide that there
(in)

potevano affogare tutte le verità della nostra santa
(they) could drown all the truth of our saintly
(all of)

religione.
religion

"Sentiamola, poichè la sapete."
Let's hear it since it (you) know

13　Un Regalo alla Sposa

"Quel povero Battistino io l'ho conosciuto. Gli portavo
That poor Battistino I him have known (For) Him (I) carried

la legna ogni settimana e so che gli affari non gli
the wood each week and (I) know that the affari not (for) him
(business)

andavan male anche con quattro figliuoli. L'uno fa oggi
went bad also with four sons The one does today
(is)

il contrabbandiere colla Svizzera, una vita da ladri,
the smuggler with the Switzerland a life of thieves
() (with)

sapete, e dice che un giorno o l'altro metterà lui la
(you) know and (he) says that one day or the other will put he the

dinamite al Zoccolino."
dynamite to the Zoccolino

"Fu lui che gli toccò staccare suo padre dal portone
(It) Was he that it touched detach his father from the door
[had to] (take down after suicide by hanging)

quella mattina, ed è un fegato sano che non ha
that morning and (he) is a liver healthy that does not have

paura del buio."
fear of the dark

14   Un Regalo alla Sposa

"Che cosa c'entra il Carpigna che ha sempre negoziato
What thing there involved the Carpigna that has always dealt
()

di carbone?"
of coal
(in)

"C'entra che Battistino gli aveva prestato sessantamila
This involved that Battistino him had loaned sixty
(This involved him)

lire, sulla parola e che il Carpigna negò di averle
lire on the word and that the Carpigna denied of to have them
(on his) () ()

ricevute mai. Ecco come c'entra."
received ever See how it involved
(it involved him)

"Fu una bestia a fidarsi."
(He) was a beast to trust oneself

"L'aveva tenuto a battesimo, pareva un santo a vederlo
He had held a baptism seemed a saint to see him

in chiesa, quando pregava la croce sull'altare."
in church when (he) prayed the cross on the altar

15 Un Regalo alla Sposa

"Son peggio degli altri."
(They) are worse of the others
(than the)

"Quello fu il principio della sua fortuna."
That was the beginning of the his fortune
(of)

Dall'altra parte del lago si gridava invece: Viva la
From the other part of the lake themselves shouted instead Live the
(side) [they shouted] (Long live)

sposa! viva gli sposi! viva il signor Gaspare!
bride live the spouses live the sir Gaspare
(long live) (long live) ()

C'erano trenta o quaranta persone, tra invitati, parenti,
There were thirty or forty people between invited relatives

barcaiuoli e persone di servizio.
boatmen and people of service

16 Un Regalo alla Sposa

Nel salone di mezzo a pianterreno, aperto sul giardino,
In the salon of (the) middle on (the) ground floor opened on the garden
(in)

la tavola preparata per la baldoria luccicava di
the table prepared for the revelry glistened of

bicchieri, di trionfi di vetro, di confetti, senza dir nulla
glasses of triumphs of glass of confetti without to say nothing
(beautiful objects)

delle torte, dei marzapani, delle gelatine, che avevano
of the pies of marzipan of the jellies that (they) had

fatto venire da Locarno.
let come from Locarno

Sopra una scansìa presso il muro una batteria di
On top of a shelf at the wall one battery of

bottiglie dal collo d'argento aspettava il momento di
bottles from neck of silver expected the moment of
(with) the

scendere in battaglia.
to descend into battle

18 Un Regalo alla Sposa

Dal giardino ogni soffio più vivo del vento portava
From the garden each breeze more lively of the wind carried

dentro un profumo acuto di limoni misto al profumo
inside a scent acute of lemons mixed to the scent

caldo delle vaniglie e dei gelsomini.
warm of the vanillas and of the jasmine

Isolina, bella, allegra, saltellava come una gattina nella
Isolina beautiful cheerful hopping as a kitten in the (in)

sua innocente giovinezza, finchè tutti sedettero a tavola
her innocent youth until everyone sat down at (the) table

e fu stappata la prima bottiglia di vin bianco d'Asti,
and (there) was uncorked the first bottle of wine white of Asti

che inondò della sua spuma d'argento l'abitino della
that flooded of the (with) its foam of silver the dress of the

sposa.
bride

19 Un Regalo alla Sposa

"Viva la sposa, viva l'allegria!"
(Long) Live the bride (long) live the joy

"Viva il signor Gaspare, padre fortunato."
(Long) live the sir Gaspare father fortunate
()

"A rivederci al battesimo."
To meet again at the baptism

Gaspare Carpigna provava nel cuore la dolcezza
Gaspare Carpigna felt in the heart the sweetness

malinconica del padre che vede la figliuola spiccare il
melancholy of the father that sees the daughter leap into the

volo dal nido, ma sa che va ad essere felice.
flight from the nest but knows that goes to be happy

20 Un Regalo alla Sposa

Isolina **era** **per** **quell'uomo** **taciturno** **e** **mezzo** **selvatico,**
Isolina was voor die man taciturn and half wild

l'unico **ideale** **al** **mondo,** **e** **si** **può** **dire** **che** **i** **denari**
the only ideal to the world and one can say that the moneys
(money)

egli **li** **avesse** **radunati** **soltanto** **per** **lei.** **Era** **contento** **di**
he them had gathered only for her (He) was happy of
(it)

maritarla **bene** **e** **con** **onore.** **Caspita!** **oltre** **il** **corredo**
to marry her off well and with honor Man! beyond the trousseau
(Expression of amazement , literally 'Trip!')

le **dava** **un** **trecentomila** **lire** **sulla** **mano,** **e** **il** **resto**
her (he) gave a threehundredthousand lire on hand and the rest
() (in) the

alla **sua** **morte.**
at the his death
(at)

Il **vin** **d'Asti** **e** **il** **vecchio** **Barolo** **di** **dodici** **anni** **non**
The wine of Asti and the old Barolo of twelve years not

furono **versati** **nel** **lago.**
were poured in the lake

21 Un Regalo alla Sposa

L'allegria   come   avvien   sempre   in   queste   circostanze,   un
The joy   such as   happens   always   in   these   circumstances   a
(avvien; apocopic -no final sound- form of avviene)

po'   tiepida   e   sconnessa   in   principio,   cominciò   subito   a
bit   lukewarm   and   disconnected   in   beginning   began   immediately   to
(at)   (the start)

levare   il   bollore.
rise   the   ardor

Gli   spiriti   fremevano   come   pentole   a   buon   fuoco.
The   spirits   shook   such as   pots   at   (a) good   fire
(minds)

A   destra   e   a   sinistra   del   viale   splendevano   le
At   right   and   at   left   of the   avenue   shone   the
(At the)   (at the)

ghirlande   dei   palloncini,   un   rosso,   l'altro   verde,   l'altro
garlands   of the   balloons   one   red   the other   green   the other
(the)

bianco,   come   una   bandiera   d'Italia.
white   such as   a   flag   of Italy

22 Un Regalo alla Sposa

Dal lago veniva sulle onde l'onda d'una serenata
From the lake came on the waves the wave of a serenade
(the soundwave)

strimpellata in un canotto a palloncini gialli, e già il
strummed in a dinghy to balloons yellow and already the
(with)

segretario comunale col calice in mano, cogli occhietti
secretary municipal with the chalice in hand with the eyes

umidi, stava per leggere una poesia, quando entrò il
moist was about to read a poem when entered the

fattore che aveva una cassettina in mano, chiusa,
steward that had a little box in (the) hand enclosed

piegata in una carta e suggellata.
folded in a paper and sealed

"L'ha portato un uomo,"
It has brought a man

"Un altro regalo per la sposa,"
An other gift for the bride

23 Un Regalo alla Sposa

"Dàlla qui, Pietro."
Give it here Pietro

Isolina prese la cassettina, e pensando subito a una
Isolina took the little box and thinking immediately to a
[of a friend of

sua amica di Luino, la collocò sulla tavola, tagliò i
her friend from Luino it placed on the table cut the
her]

suggelli col coltellino d'argento, spiegò la carta che
seals with the boxcutter of silver laid out the paper that

l'involgeva. Era una cassettina rettangolare, di legno di
it wrapped It was one little box rectangular of wood of

pino, come si usa per i pettini, rustica, bianca con
pine such as one uses for the combs rustic white with

su scritto: Alla sposa.
on written To the bride
(on it)

Isolina   l'aprì   con   quella   viva   curiosità   che   eccitano   le
Isolina   opened it   with   that   lively   curiosity   that   cause   the

cose   misteriose.
things   mysterious

Vide   una   lettera,   e   sotto   dei   frastagli   di   carta   a   vari
(She) Saw   a   letter   and   beneath   of the   indentations   of   paper   with   varying
()

colori,   con   riccioli   d'oro,   e   più   sotto,   uno   strato   di
colors   with   ringlets   of gold   and   most   beneath   a   layer   of

crusca.
bran
(filling material)

"Segretario,   legga   lei   la   lettera,"   disse   Isolina   senza
Secretary   read   you   the   letter   said   Isolina   without

guardarla.
looking at it

25 Un Regalo alla Sposa

Il segretario lasciò via il sonetto, prese l'altro foglio e
The secretary put away the sonnet took the other sheet and

con quella medesima intonazione, a cui aveva già
with that same intonation to which (he) had already

preparata la bocca....
prepared the mouth

Dirò prima che l'attenzione degli astanti era stata
(I) Will say before that the attention of the bystanders was been (had)

richiamata sulla cassettina dal vedere Isolina che vi
called back to the little box of the () to see Isolina that (who) (in) it

rimestava colle mani, e ne traeva della crusca,
stirred with the hands and from it drew of the () bran

ponendola di mano in mano sul piatto assieme ai
placing from hand in (to) hand on the plate together to the (with the)

confetti.
confetti

26 Un Regalo alla Sposa

Il segretario lesse dunque, anzi declamò: "A Gaspare
The secretary read therefore indeed (he) declaimed To Gaspare

Carpigna, lettera dell'altro mondo."
Carpigna (a) letter from the other world

A tutti parve una frase comica e pazza fatta per
To everyone (this) seemed a sentence comical and crazy made for

ridere; chi rise, chi alzò la mano, chi il bicchiere.
to laugh who laughed who rose the hand who the glass
(this one) (that one) (another one)

E il segretario, distratto come un'oca e colla testa
And the secretary distracted as a goose and with the head

piena di fumo continuò: "Carpigna, alla dote di tua
full of smoke continued Carpigna to the dowry of your

figlia aggiungi anche la collana di Battistino dell'Oro."
daughter (I) add as well the necklace of Battistino dell'Oro

27 Un Regalo alla Sposa

Tutto ciò fu letto come un sonetto, nel tempo che
All this was read such as a sonnet in the time that

l'Isolina colle manine bianche e piene di diamanti
the Isolina with the hands white and full of diamonds

traeva dalla crusca una cordicella nera, grumosa, grossa
drew from the bran a thin rope black lumpy thick

come il suo dito mignolo, lunga come una vipera
as the her finger pinky long as a viper
  ()

comune, che, inorridita, lei lasciò cadere, che parve
common that horrified she let fall that seemed

proprio una biscia morta. Gettò un grido, storcendo la
truly a snake dead (She) uttered a cry twisting the

bocca, alzando le due mani colle dita rigide, adunche,
mouth raising the both hands with the fingers stiff hooked
  ()

mentre un silenzio profondo, un silenzio brutale, un
while a silence deep a silence brutal a

silenzio di ghiaccio sottentrò alla festa.
silence of ice under-entered the party

E cento occhi bianchi, cento occhi gelati si fissavano
And hundred eyes white hundred eyes cold themselves fixed

sul viso incartapecorito del signor Gaspare. Un buffo
at the face turned into parchment of the sir Gaspare A breeze
(turned a deathly pale) (of)

d'aria stortò le fiamme delle candele.
of air twisted the flames of the candles

La sposa fu portata via. Quando andarono a risvegliare
The bride was carried away When (they) went to awaken

dal suo deliquio il signor Gaspare, ch'era rimasto colla
from the his swoon the sir Gaspare who was remained with the
(from) () (fixed)

pupilla di vetro sulla biscia morta, gli trovarono le
pupil of glass on the snake dead him (they) found the

mani fredde, i piedi lunghi e la bocca piena di
hands cold the feet long and the mouth full of
(stretched)

sangue. Soltanto i capelli parevano vivi sul capo.
blood Only the hair seemed alive on the head

29 Un Regalo alla Sposa

Intanto sull'alto picco della Zeda, un contrabbandiere
Meanwhile on the top peak of the Zeda a smuggler

sfidava il buio fischiando, cantando:
challenged the dark whistling singing

"Sposettina, vien con me..."
Little bride come with me

NEI BOSCHI
IN THE WOODS

Chi non conosce i boschi dell'alto Milanese, detti
Who not knows the woods of the high Milanese (the) said

boschi di Saronno, di Mombello, di Limbiate, può
woods of Saronno of Mombello of Limbiate can

immaginare una stesa di selve, sopra un terreno
imagine a stretch of forests on a terrain
(stesa; short for distesa)

disuguale, una volta incolto e oggi piantato a pini
unequal one time uncultivated and today planted to pines
(with)

silvestri e a qualche rovere, che è quanto la terra,
of the forest and to some oak that is how much the earth
(scottish) (with)

oltre le eriche e il bruco, può sopportare.
beyond the heather and the caterpillar can bear

Queste piantagioni non sono molto antiche e appunto
These plantations not are very old and in fact

per ciò, non sono molto note.
for this not are much noted

Della maggior parte si ricordano i nostri padri d'aver
Of the most part themselves remember the our fathers of to have
(For the)   ()   ()   (to have)

veduto i primi germogli, quando ancora quel nudo tratto
seen the first shoots when yet that naked tract

di paese non era che una nuda sodaglia. Oggi il
of land not was that a naked wasteland Today the
(but)

bosco è maturo, non dirò per i ladri, che non vivono
forest is mature not (I) say for the robbers that not live
(who)

più per i boschi, ma per tutti coloro che amano le
more by the woods but for all those that love the
(anymore) (in)   (who)

meste solitudini e sognano sempre, quando sono in un
sad solitudes and dream always when (they) are in one

luogo, di trovarsi in un altro.
place of find themselves in an other
(to be)

A me questi boschi ricordano per esempio, certe
To me these woods remember for instance certain

solitudini dell'antica Caledonia:
solitudes of the ancient Caledonia

E   il   più   bello   si   è   che   in   Caledonia   non   ci   sono
And   the   most   beautiful itself is that   in   Caledonia   not   there (I) am
                               (it)   (have)

mai   stato.
ever   been

Ma   non   si   è   letto   inutilmente   a   dodici   anni   una
But   not   oneself   is   read   useless   to   twelve   years   a
               ()   (have)   (for nothing) (during)

dozzina   di   romanzi   del   Walter   Scott,   seduti   all'ombra   di
dozen   of   novels   of   Walter   Scott   seated   at   of
                                                                 (in) the shade

un'antica   quercia,   o   anche   solo   sul   pianerottolo   della
an old   oak   or   also   only   on the   landing   of the

scala.
stair
(stairs)

Se   non   è   come   in   Scozia,   vi   son   tratti   nei   boschi
If   not   (it) is like   in   Scotland   there   are   traits   in the   woods

di   Limbiate   che   potrebbero   essere   trasportati   in
of   Limbiate   that   could   be   transported   in
                                                   (latin . transponere; placed)

Scandinavia   e   allora   è   ancora   più   bello   per   chi   ama
Scandinavia   and   so   (it) is   even   more   beautiful   for   who   loves

viaggiare   a   piedi.
to travel   on   feet
                   (foot)

Le   piante   d'un   verde   scuro   perenne,   di   un   fusto
The   plants   of a   green   dark   perennial   of   a   stem

magro   e   diritto,   che   si   apre   a   larga   piuma   o   a
thin   and   straight   that   itself opens   to   wide   plume   or   to

ombrello,   collocate   a   migliaia   l'una   presso   l'altra   in   una
umbrella   placed   by   thousands   the one against   the other in   a

disposizione   quasi   simmetrica,   e   così   per   l'estensione   di
disposal   almost   symmetrical   and   as such   for   the extension   of

cinque   o   sei   miglia: i   viali   che   tagliano   questi   eserciti
five   or   six   miles   the   avenues   that   cut   these   armies

di   piante   e   si   prolungano,   si   sprofondano   nel   verde   a
of   plants   and   themselves extend   themselves collapse   in the   green   to
                                                                                        [until

perdita   d'occhio: le   forre   di   altissime   erbe   filiformi   dove
loss   of eye   the   ravines   of   high   herbs   whiskery   where
out of   eyesight]

non   entrano   che   i   bracchi: la   terra   gialla,   rotta   da
do not   come   that   the   hounds   the   ground   yellow   broken   from
                    (but)

immensi   crepacci   dove   la   picchia   il   sole:
immense   crevasses   where   it   beats   the   sun

Molle,   melmosa,   scivolante   come   il   sapone   dove   l'acqua
Soft   muddy   slippery   such as the   soap   where   the water

stagna: gli   scoli   d'acqua   piovana   che   scendono   a
stands still the   drains   of water   rain   that   descends   to
                               [rainwater   ]

formare   pozze,   paludi,   laghetti,   e   fin   dei   laghettoni
form   puddles   marshes   ponds   and   at last of the   little lakes
                                                                        ()

perenni   circondati   da   conifere   con   increspature   e   piccole
year round   surrounded   by   conifers   with   ripples   and   small

tempeste   sconosciute   al   mondo,   come   quelle   delle
storms   unknown   to the world   such as those   of the

anime   modeste: e   poi   aggiungete   un   silenzio   profondo,
souls   modest   and   then   (you) add   a   silence   deep

non   interrotto   nemmeno   dal   solito   stormire   delle   fronde
not   interrupted   even   from the usual   rustling   of the   fronds

(il   pino   è   taciturno) e   i   chiarori   celestiali   e   mistici
the   pine   is   taciturn   and   the   clearings   heavenly   and   mystics

dell'aria   al   disopra   di   tanto   verde,   e   le   fiamme   vaganti
of the air   to the above   of   much   green   and   the   flames   straying
(of the open air) (of the)

del   tramonto   veduto   attraverso   alle   fessure   del   bosco....
of the sunset   seen   through   to the   cracks   of the forest
                                               (the)

Tutto ciò voglio dire, mi ha tante volte trasportato
All this (I) want to say me has many times transported

fuori di me in una regione dove io sento che son
outside of myself in a region where I feel that am (I have)

vissuto un'altra volta, forse diecimila anni fa.
lived another time maybe ten thousand years ago

Oh la poesia, amici, è pur la dolcissima cosa!
Oh the poetry friends is really the sweetest thing

Voi uscite un mattino d'autunno, con un libro, mettiamo
You exit one morning of autumn with a book (we) take

Aleardo Aleardi, nella tasca del carniere, col fucile ad
Aleardo Aleardi in the pocket of the game bag with the rifle to

armacollo, col vostro cane che vi saltella innanzi, girate
shoulder with your dog that yourself jumps in front turn

dietro le case, pigliate verso il cimitero vecchio, date
behind the homes pick up towards the cemetery old give (take)

un'occhiata a quei poveri morti e a quella croce
a little eye at those poor dead and at that cross
(a look)

bianca dove da cinquant'anni dorme una contessina
white where from fifty years sleeps a Countess
(since)

morta...
dead

37 Nei Boschi

No, no, non è poesia.
No no not (it) is poetry

Io fui innamorato a sedici anni di quella contessina,
I was in love at sixteen years of that Countess
                                      (with)

ed è una storia che ho promesso di contare qualche
and (it) is a story that (I) have promised of to recount some
                                                    ()

volta.
time

Io l'ho seguita attraverso alle ombre del bosco, più
I her have followed through to the shadows of the forest more
                                  (the)

contento quanto più le nebbie del novembre entravano
happy how much more the mists of the November entered
       (when)   (of)

fra le piante a rannuvolare i contorni della selva.
between the plants to cloud the contours of the wilderness

Una   mattina,   giusto   sui   primi   di   novembre,   mentre   io
One   morning   right   at the   firsts   of   November   while   I
(beginning)

correvo   prima   di   colazione   attraverso   la   pineta,
hurried   before   of   breakfast   through   the   pine forest
()

pensando   al   mio   futuro   poema   sulla   *Risurrezione*   *dei*
thinking   to the   my   future   poem   about   *Resurrection*   *of the*
(to)

Morti,   fui   a   un   tratto   arrestato   da   una   fiamma   che   si
Dead   (I) was   at   a   stroke   stopped   because of a   flame   that   itself
[suddenly   ]

agitava   in   fondo,   e   che   stentava   quasi   a   rompere   il
stirred   in   (the) background   and   that   struggled   almost   to   break   the

velo   bianco   e   gelato   dalla   nebbia.
veil   (of) white   and   ice   from the   fog

Anche   *Pill*,   il   mio   cane   da   caccia,   si   fermò   su
Also   *Pill*   the   my   dog   of   hunting   itself   stopped   at
[my   hunting   dog   ]   ()

quattro   piedi,   col   muso   in   alto,   e   la   piccola   coda
four   paws   with the   muzzle   in   high   and   the   small   tail
()

piena   di   meraviglia.
full   of   wonder

La Cherubina mi aveva detto prima ch'io uscissi di
The Cherubina me had told before that I went out from

casa che si sarebbe fatta colazione alle undici, più
(the) house that itself would be made breakfast at the eleven more
                      (there)   (at) (o'clock) [later

tardi del solito, perchè si aspettava mio fratello coi
later of the usual because themselves expected my brother with the
]   (than)   (there were)

parenti della sposa.
relatives of the wife

Da due giorni si lavorava in cucina a preparare quella
Since two days herself worked in kitchen to prepare that
                                    (the kitchen)

colazione, che doveva essere un banchetto di
breakfast that had to be a banquet of

Sardanapalo con un piatto di selvaggina e un brodo
Sardanapalo with a plate of game and a broth
(Assyrian king)

ristretto che pareva giulebbe.
concentrated that seemed julep
                           (Italian sweet drink of boiled fruits)

L'importanza   d'una   casa   si   conosce   a   tavola   e   mio
The importance   of a   house   one   knows   by   table   and   my
(the dish)

padre   voleva,   come   si   dice,   far   colpo   su   della   gente
father   wanted   as   one   says   make   strike   on   of the   people
(an impression)   (the)

un   po'   materiale....   Ma   sono   cose   che   non   hanno
a   bit   material   But   (those) are   things   that   not   have

nulla   a   che   fare   con   quella   fiamma   che,   come   ho
nothing   to   that   do   with   that   flame   that   as   (I) have
(anything)   ()

detto,   si   agitava   in   fondo   al   bosco   e   che   stentava
said   itself   stirred   in   back   to the   forest   and   that   struggled
()   (of the)

quasi   a   rompere   il   velo   fitto   della   nebbia.
almost   to   break   the   veil   thick   of the   fog

Strano   un   fuoco   nei   nostri   boschi!   Man   mano   che   io
Strange   a   fire   in the   our   woods   Hand   hand   that   I
(in)   [bit by bit   ]   (while)

mi   avvicinavo,   la   fiamma   si   faceva   più   distinta,   e   già
myself   approached   the   flame   itself   was making   more   distinct   and   already

si   potevano   vedere   nel   chiarore   rosso   del   fuoco
one   could   see   in the   flare   red   of the   fire

disegnarsi   alcune   figure   radunate   in   cerchio   come   a   un
draw themselves   some   figures   gathered   in   circle   such as   to   a
(be visible)   (of)

tristo   complotto   di   negromanti.
sad   conspiracy   of   necromancers

41 Nei Boschi

La solitudine e la selvatichezza del luogo che
The loneliness and the wildness of the place that

s'internava in una specie di crocicchio: quelle ombre
itself wrapped in a sort of crossroads those shadows

ballonzolanti sul fusto delle piante al mobile ed acceso
bobbing on the stem of the plants to the mobile and turned on

riflesso della fiamma fumosa e resinosa, avrebbero ben
reflection of the flame smoky and resinous would well

potuto far credere a un convegno di malviventi, se
was able to make believe to a convening of criminals if

dopo alcuni passi non avessi riconosciuto le gambe
after some steps not (I) had recognized the legs

lunghe e magre del signor segretario comunale, e
long and lean of the (of) mr secretary municipal and

accanto a lui la figura tozza del console e due o
next to him the figure squat of the consul and two or

tre guardie campestri.
three guards rural

Il console s'era seduto in adorazione del fuoco sopra
The consul himself was sat (was) (sitting) in worship of the fire on

un pezzo di tronco.
a piece of (tree)trunk

42   Nei Boschi

Battistino, una delle guardie campestri con un ginocchio
Battistino one of the guards rural with a knee

a terra cercava di far saltare un carbone acceso nel
on (the) ground sought of to make jump a coal lighted in the
(tried) ()

buco della pipa, mentre il signor Boltracchi, il
hole of the pipe while the mr Boltracchi the
()

segretario, scaldava le parti meno rispettabili della sua
secretary warmed the parts less respectable of the his
(of)

persona, voltando le spalle al focolare, colle gambe
person turning the shoulders to the fireplace with the legs

aperte come un compasso.
spread like a compass

Quella brava gente si trovava da qualche ora nel
Those good people themselves found since some time in the
(found themselves)

bosco e col freddo del novembre e coll'erba bagnata
forest and with the cold of the november and with the grass wet
(of)

di guazza, sentiva volontieri il beneficio d'una scaldatina.
of dew felt willingly the benefit of a warming up

43 Nei Boschi

Il console quando mi vide, toccò l'orlo del cappello
The consul when me (he) saw touched the edge of the hat

colle due dita e disse:
with the two fingers and said
(with)

"Riverisco, sor avvocato."
Revere sir lawyer
(I revere you; polite expression)

Il buon uomo era un mio contadino e nella sua
The good man was a my farmer and in the his
[a farmer of mine] (in)

semplicità sentiva un grande rispetto della mia persona.
simplicity felt a great respect of the my person
(of)

"Che cosa fate, la polenta?" domandai.
What thing make the polenta (I) asked
() (do you make) (polenta; grain- or cornmeal porridge)

"È per cagione di quel Gasparino della Vela," rispose
(It) is by cause of that Gasparino of the Vela answered
[because]

il console con quel linguaggio lungo che è proprio
the consul with that language long which is aspect
(typical)

dell'alto Milanese.
of the high Milanese

"Che cosa ha fatto Gasparino della Vela?"
What thing has made Gasparino of the Vela
()

"È morto."
(He) is dead

"Era malato?"
(He) Was ill

"Da un mese, sor avvocato, un poco di pellagra, ma
Since a month sir lawyer a little of pellagra but
(*skin affliction*)

bisogna dire che gli sia andata ai visceri del capo."
necessary to say that him (it) shall be gone to the insides of the head

"Se non ho sentito a suonare l'agonia."
If not (I) have heard to play the agony
(But) (the bell tolling)

"Si muore anche senza la campana," interruppe
You die also without the bell interrupted

Battistino colle parole mozze di chi ha in bocca una
Battistino with the words cut off of who has in (the) mouth a

pipa corta che gli abbrucia quasi le palpebre.
pipe short that him scorched almost the eyelids

45 Nei Boschi

Il signor Boltracchi mi accennò col pollice sopra la
The sir Boltracchi me pointed at with the thumb above the
()

spalla qualche cosa alla sua destra. Guardai e vidi il
shoulder some thing to the his right (I) looked and (I) saw the
(to) ()

mio *Pill* quasi stecchito sulle sue quattro gambe, che
my *Pill* almost dead on the his four legs who
(on)

tremava tutto sotto la sua pelle.
trembled wholly beneath the his pelt
()

A un nuovo cenno del Boltracchi feci un mezzo giro
At a new sign of the Boltracchi (I) made a half turn
(of)

sopra di me, guardai indietro presso le piante e allora
on of me (I) looked back at the plants and then
(myself)

scorsi sul terreno molle per la pioggia del dì prima,
past on the ground soft for the rain of the day before
(that)

un non so che, coperto da una stuoia di carro e
a not (I) know what covered by a mat of wagon and

da una gualdrappa logora, e sotto un po' di paglia.
by a mantle worn and beneath a bit of straw

Da uno dei lati uscivano due piedi lunghi, magri,
From one of the sides came out two feet long thin
(ends)

infangati, colle unghie lunghe, due brutti piedi che
muddy with the nails long two ugly feet that

parevano quelli della morte, i piedi insomma del morto.
seemed those of the dead the feet in short of the dead man

"O Dio, che cosa è stato?"
Oh God what thing is happened
()

Il console stendendo le sue mani alla fiamma, continuò
The consul stretching the his hands to the flame continued
()

col suo tono naturale:
with the his tone natural

"Gli è venuta addosso la scalmana, si vede.
Him is come over the craze one sees
(has) (can see)

Stamattina, la va bene?"
This morning it goes fine
(went)

47   Nei Boschi

"Mentre la sua donna era a messa aprì l'uscio,
While the his woman was to mass (he) opened the door
()

traversò l'orto e nudo come è uscito dal ventre della
crossed the garden and naked such as (he) is come out from the belly of the
(has) (womb) (of)

sua mamma, prese la via dei boschi."
his mother took the way of the woods

"Dev'essere passato dal laghettone di Mombello."
(He) Must be passed of the little lake of Mombello
(have) (by the)

"Ci sarebbe rimasto, se fosse passato, perchè l'acqua
There (he) would be remained if (he) was passed why the water
(have) (had)

è alta. Invece si vede che ha traversato il vallone
is high Instead one sees that (he) has crossed the valley

della Merla, si è cacciato nei boschi vecchi di
of Merla himself is hunted in the woods old of

Lenzano e andò a finire alla pozza del Vetro. Qui
Lenzano and went to end at puddle of the Glass Here
(in) the

ha creduto di poter traversare, ma c'è rimasto preso
(he) has believed of to be able to cross but there is remained taken

al vischio."
to sticky
(by) the (mud)

"C'è   una   terra   che   par   giusto   liscivia."
It is   a   land   that   by   right   cleans
            [truly   ]

"Son   passato   ieri   dalla   pozza   del   Vetro   e   non   c'era
(I) am   passed   yesterday   from the   puddle   of   Glass   and   not   there was
(have)

un   barile   d'acqua."
a   barrel   of water

"Ne   è   venuta   un   poco   stanotte."
There   is   come   a   little   tonight
      (has)

"Si   è   mandato   ad   avvisare   il   sindaco   e   il   maresciallo,"
One   is   sent   to   advise   the   mayor   and   the   marshal
      (has)   (warn)

disse   il   segretario   voltandosi   davanti   alla   fiamma.
said   the   secretary   turning himself   towards   to the   flame

"Non   era   vostro   parente?"   dimandò   Battistino   al   console.
Not   was   your   relative   asked   Battistino   to the   consul

49   Nei Boschi

"Ha sposato una mia sorella, sicchè lascia tre figliuoli.
(He) Has married a my sister so that (he) leaves three sons
[a sister of mine]

Uno è soldato."
One is soldier

"Adesso potrà venire a casa, se è morto il vecchio..."
Now (he) will be able to come to house if (he) is dead the old man
[home]

"La legge non permette se non ci sono dei
The law not permits if not there are of the
()

minorenni," disse gravemente il signor Boltracchi.
minors said seriously the mr Boltracchi

Pill, coll'unghie tese, col muso avanti, rigido come un
Pill with the paws strained with the muzzle forward rigid as a

cane di legno, non cessava di fiutare il morto.
dog of wood not ceased of to sniff the dead

"Lo sa la sua donna?"
It knows the his woman
        ()   (wife)

"Quando è tornata dalla messa che era ancora bujo,
When is returned from the mass that was still dark
     (she had)   (it)

verso le cinque, la va bene? trovò l'uscio aperto.
towards the five it goes fine found the door opened
          (o'clock) [about]   (she found)

Allora capì che il suo Gasparino era scappato, perchè
Then understood that the her Gasparino was escaped because
     (she understood) ()

aveva tentato un'altra volta, di scappare. Si mise a
(he) had attempted another time of to escape Herself put to
                                      ()   [She started]

gridare, a chiamar gente. Venne un ragazzo dei
shout to call people It was a boy of the

Melgoni a dire che aveva veduto un uomo nudo
Melgoni to say that (he) had seen a man naked

come un verme che correva nei boschi e che era
as a worm that ran in the woods and that was

Gasparino della Vela. Allora si è cominciato a cercare
Gasparino of the Vela Then themselves began to search
                           (one) (has)

nel bosco e si sono trovati dei passi freschi colla
in the forest and themselves are found of the steps fresh with the
                  (there)   (footprints)

pianta delle dita."
plant of the fingers

"Cerca di qua, cerca di là, poi abbiamo incontrato voi
Search of here search of there then (we) have encountered you
() ()

Battistino, la va bene?"
Battistino it goes fine
[is that correct?]

"Io venivo da Bovisìo, dov'ero stato a portare un paio
I came from Bovisio where was been to bring a pair
(where I had)

di stivali al calzolaio, perchè mi mettesse le calcagna
of boots to the shoemaker (that's why) I put the heels
[started off]

e giungo alla pozza del Vetro, quando mi par di
and reached the puddle of Glass when me seemed of

sentire un scialacquamento come fa il mio cane
to hear a splashing such as makes the my dog
()

quando ha caldo ed entra nella pozza a lavare le
when has hot and enters in the pool to wash the
(he is)

pulci. Ho creduto anzi che fosse il *Pill* del signor
fleas (I) had believed indeed that (it) was the *Pill* of the sir
() (of)

avvocato, che viene volentieri incontro quando sa che
lawyer that comes willingly meeting when (he knows that)

vado per i boschi. Anzi mi fermai e chiamai forte:
(I) go through the woods Indeed I stopped and (I) called forcefully

'Pill '..."
Pill

"Torno   a   sentire   un   'ciuf-ciuf'   nell'acqua."
(I) returned   to   hear   a   splash-splash   in the water
(repeated)

"'Pill!   dove   sei?'   ...   e   fischio,   così....   mentre   vado
Pill   where   are   and   whistled   like this   while   (I) go
(you)

verso   la   pozza   dietro   il   rumore..."
towards   the   puddle   after   the   noise

Battistino,   prese   la   pipa   colla   sinistra,   e   mandò   un
Battistino   took   the   pipe   with the   left   and   sent   a

sibilo   acuto   da   cacciatore   che   risuonò   per   tutta   la
whistle   piercing   from   hunter   that   rang out   throughout   whole   the

solitudine.   L'altro   villano,   che   non   aveva   mai   parlato   e
loneliness   The other   lout   that   not   had   ever   spoken   and

che   conobbi   per   il   Rosso,   sorrise   colla   sua   faccia
that   (I) knew   for   the   Red   smiled   with the   his   face
(as)   (with)   [his   idiotic frog

cretina   di   ranocchio.
idiotic   of   frog
face   ]

"'Pill'.... Non sentendo più nulla, vado giù verso la
Pill — Not — hearing — (any)more — nothing — (I) go — down — towards — the

pozza e trovo quel povero cristiano in un boccale
puddle — and — find — that — poor — christian — in — a — mug (ful)

d'acqua tutto impastato come un mostro nella melma,
of water — totally — pasted — as — a — monster — in the — slime

che aveva trovato la maniera di annegare."
that (so) — (he) had — found — the — manner — of — to drown

"È la pellagra che mette una sete d'inferno."
(It) Is — the — pellagra (skin disease) — that — puts (causes) — a — thirst — of hell

"Capita spesso alla bassa che i malati si buttano nel
(It) Happens — often — at the — low (worst period) — that — the — sick — themselves — throw — in the

pozzo."
well

"Vi sarete spaventato, Battistino."
You — would be — scared — Battistino

55 Nei Boschi

"Non è la prima volta. L'anno scorso vi ricordate quel
Not (it) is the first time The year gone you remember that
(past)

matto di Mombello che scappò dallo stabilimento e che
madman of Mombello that escaped from the establishment and that
(institute)

s'impiccò fra due piante? L'ho visto pel primo una
hanged himself between both plants Him seen as the first one
(trees) (I) have

mattina di gennaio."
morning of january

"Era arrampicato sopra un pino altissimo dove attaccò
(He) was climbed on a pine high where (he) attached
(had) (in)

la corda; poi andò sopra un'altra pianta più alta e
the rope then (he) went on another plant most high and
(in) (tree)

attaccò l'altro capo, e Dio sa come potè impiccarsi a
attached the other head and God knows how (he) could hang himself at
(end)

mezz'aria all'altezza d'un campanile."
midair at the height of a bell tower

"I matti hanno una gran forza."
The mad have a large force

"M'è toccato vederlo tra il chiaro e il fosco. Il freddo
Me is   touched   to see him   between the   clear   and   the   dark   The   cold
[It   happened to me]   (sky)

aveva gelata anche la corda e il matto pareva di
had   frozen   also   the   rope   and   the   madman   seemed   of

vetro."
glass

"La Bortola del sarto ha vinto cinquantasei lire coi
The   Bortola   of the   tailor   has   won   fifty-six   lire   with the
[Bortola , the wife of   the   tailor]

numeri del matto."
numbers   of the   madman

Il Rosso rise ancora gonfiando gli occhi slavati.
The   Red   laughed   again   swelling   the   eyes   washed out

"Quello era un conte diventato matto per i liquori."
That   was   a   count   (that had) become   crazy   because of the   liquors

57   Nei Boschi

"Chi troppo, chi nulla..."
This one too much that one nothing

"C'è qui il maresciallo."
There is here the marshal

Venne anche il sindaco e il dottore. Il cadavere fu
Came too the mayor and the Doctor The corpse was

scoperto. Pareva una mummia ingiallita. La creta gli
uncovered (It) Seemed a mummy yellowed The clay it

riempiva ancora la bocca e i forellini del naso.
filled still the mouth and the holes of the nose

Pill pareva diventato di sasso e guardava il morto con
Pill seemed (to have) become of stone and looked at the dead with

occhio lagrimoso.
eye tearful

Povero Gasparino! lo si sarebbe detto un fossile di
Poor Gasparino it one would be said a fossil of
(would have)

tremila anni, e nel suo freddo abbandono non si
three thousand years and in the its cold abandonment not itself
(in)

scorgeva che una tenue espressione d'ironia agli spigoli
saw that a small expression of irony on the edges
(but)

della bocca. Non era certo la creta che lo faceva
of the mouth Not was surely the clay that him made

ridere.
laugh

Pill mangiò poco quel giorno.
Pill ate little that day

59   Nei Boschi

AI TEMPI DEI TEDESCHI
At the times   of   (the) Germans
                            (1798 to 1866 , Venice and Padua part of Austria)

"Tutte le   mattine la   salutavo   con   un   bel   trillo   di
All   the mornings her (I) greeted with a   beautiful melody of

flauto   (allora il   flauto   era di   moda) : e   tutte le   sere,
(the) flute then   the flute   was of   fashion and all   the evenings
                                       (in)

prima di   levarmi   le   scarpe, le   mandavo   un   altro   saluto
before of   to take me off the shoes   her (I) sent an   other   salute

con   una volatina di   note,   che   volevan dire: 'Bona
with a   flight   of   notes   that wanted   to say   Good

note, siora Nina!'"
night lady   Nina

"Lei, insomma,   era innamorato della   sua vicina."
She   in summary   was loved   by the her neighbor
       (in short)   (by)

"Come un   angelo, ero   innamorato."
Like   an   angel   (I) was   in love

"A vent'anni l'amore va tutto in fiore, e quando la
At twenty years the love goes all in bloom and when the

sorte ti mette accanto a una bella donnina, il meno
fate you puts next to a beautiful young lady the least

che si possa fare è di farle la corte col flauto."
that one can do is of to make her the courtship with the flute

"E il marito?"
And the husband

"Il marito d'una bella donnina è sempre un brutto
The husband of a beautiful young lady is always an ugly

mostro, un tiranno, uno scimmiotto, questo si sa. Nel
monster a tyrant a monkey this one knows In the
(baboon)

caso mio, il sior Malgoni, imp. reg. impiegato alla
case (of) mine the mr Malgoni imp . reg . employee to the
[imperial regal accountant

contabilità, un omaccione linfatico e geloso, meritava
accounting a big man lymphatic and jealous (he) deserved
] (showing veins)

qualche riguardo."
some care
(caution)

"Prima perchè in fondo voleva bene a sua moglie, e
First because in bottom (he) wished well to his wife and
(basically)

poi perchè aveva delle amicizie in polizia e a quei
then because (he) had of the friendships in (the) police and at those
() (in)

tempi non c'era troppo a fidarsi. Parlo dei tempi dei
times not there was too much to trust oneself (I) speak of (the) times of
(into)

tedeschi."
(the) Germans

"Ho capito. Lei non andava più in là del flauto."
(I) Have understood You not went further in that of the flute

"Ero un matricolino sui vent'anni, un pò' timido, come
(I) Was a registered on the twenty years a bit timid like
(freshman) (of) (shy)

chi non è mai uscito dal suo guscio. Qualche volta
who not is never went out from the his shell Some time
(has) [now and then]

mi arrischiavo di gridare dalla finestra: 'La se péttena,
me (I) risked of to call from the window There yourself comb

siora Nina! vol piovere? vol far belo, siora Nina?'"
lady Nina will rain will make beautiful lady Nina
(will it) (will it) (be) (weather)

"E   la   siora   Nina?"
And the lady   Nina

"'Sì,   sior   Anzolo,   vol   piovere,   vol   far   bel   tempo! ... '"
Yes   sir   Anzolo   (it) will rain   (it) will make beautiful weather
                                                    (be)

"Un'arcadia!"
An arcadia
(countryside paradise)

"E   non   mancavano   i   sonetti."
And not   lacked   the sonnets

"Anche   i   sonetti?"
Also   the sonnets

"Sicuro;   li   stampavo   sul   *Trovatore*:"
Sure   them (I) printed on the *Trovatore*
                                        (Seeker)

"Un   giornaletto   teatrale   di   Padova,   e   glieli   facevo
A   journal   theatrical of   Padua   and   her them   (I) made

pervenire   con   delle   iniziali   molto   trasparenti.   Seppi
to reach   with   of the   initials   very   transparent   (I) Knew
                      ()   (clear)

più tardi   che   la   siora   Nina   non   sapeva   leggere   più   in
more late   that   the   lady   Nina   not   knew   to read   more   in
(later)

là   del   suo   libro   da   messa;   ma   le   donne,   quando
that   of the   her   book   from   mass   but   the   women   when
       (than)   (service)

amano,   son   come   i   gatti;   ci   vedono   anche   al   buio.
(they) love are   like   the   cats   us   (they) see also   at the dark
                                                                         (in the)

Suo   marito   se   l'era   tirata   in   casa   ancor   ragazzina,
Her   husband   himself   her was   pulled   in   house   still   child
                              (her he had) (taken)

con   una   gonnella   di   cotone   e   un   paio   di   zoccoli   sui
with   a   little skirt   of   cotton   and   a   pair   of   wooden shoes on the

piedi;   l'aveva   mandata   a   scuola   un   po'   di   tempo   dalle
feet   her had   sent   to   school   a   bit   of   time   of the
          [he had sent her]   (with the)

monache,   e   quando   la   servetta   gli   parve   cresciuta
nuns   and   when   the   maid   him   seemed   grown

abbastanza,   se   l'era   sposata   per   avere   una   compagna
enough   himself   her was   married   for   to have   a   companion
                          (her had)

fedele.   Il   poveretto,   più   vecchio   una   ventina   d'anni,
faithful   The   poor guy   more   old   one   twenty   of years
                                [older   ]   ()   (years)

pativa   d'asma   e   di   mal   di   cuore."
suffered   from asthma   and   of   (a) bad   of   heart
                                                        ()

"Ed è sempre prudenza aver qualcuno che ti assista
And (it) is always prudent to have someone that you assists

in un bisogno e ti faccia compagnia la notte."
in a need and (to) you makes (the) company (in) the night

"Era bella?"
Was beautiful
(Was she)

"Bellissima no, ma un musettino gustoso di servetta
(The) most beautiful not but a little snout tasty of maid
(face)

friulana, con dei riccioli biondi che incorniciavano un
Friulana with of the curls blond that framed a
(a folkdance) ()

bell'ovale colorito e sano. Gaia, spiritosa come tutte le
beautiful oval coloured and healthy Gay spirited like all the
()

nostre venete, la fortuna non l'aveva fatta salire in
our venetian women the fortune not her had made to go up in

superbia. Nella sua ignoranza aveva un fascino naturale,
pride In her ignorance (she) had a fascination natural
(enthousiasm)

non guasto dalle solite compassature del galateo sociale."
not broken down by the usual application of the etiquette social

"Gente in quella casa ce ne andava poca, tranne
People in that house there of it went little except

qualche provinciale, che capitava di tempo in tempo a
some provincial that turned up (of) time in time to

trovar la Nina diventata *parona*."
find the Nina become *mistress*
(padrona)

"L'unica persona di riguardo, che visitava con qualche
The only person of regard that visited with some
(to) (high esteem)

frequenza l'imp. reg. impiegato della contabilità era il
frequency the imp. reg. employee of accounting was the
[imperial regal accountant]

dottor Franzon, un professore della facoltà medica,
doctor Franzon a university professor of the faculty medical

compatriota del Malgoni e suo medico curante. Franzon
friend of Malgoni and his doctor curing Franzon

era già una mezza celebrità fin da quel tempo per
was already a half celebrity end of that time for
() (at)

le sue fortunate operazioni ostetriche."
the his fortunate operations obstetrical

"E la gran scienza faceva perdonare in lui il naso
And the large science made pardon (in) him the nose
(did)

d'aquilotto e i modi di villan scozzonato e superbo,
of big eagle and the ways of villain instructive and arrogant
(authoritarian)

che gli avevano meritato il titolo di dottor *Grobiàn*."
that him (they) had deserved the title of doctor *Grobian*
(fictional Saint of the rude)

"L'onore e la scienza di tanto uomo si riverberavano
The honor and the science of so much man themselves-reverberated

sulla modesta casa Malgoni, specialmente dopo che
on the modest house (of) Malgoni especially after that

Franzon era salito in auge alla Corte per una felice
Franzon was went out in height at the Court for a happy
(esteem)

operazione, che aveva salvato alla monarchia uno dei
operation that had saved to the monarchy one of the
(for the)

trecentotrentatrè arciduchini d'Austria."
333 archdukes of Austria

"E   poi   fa   sempre   comodo   d'aver   un   dottore   amico,
And   then   makes   always   comfortable   to have   a   doctor   friend
               (it is)

quando   si   soffre   d'asma   e   di   palpitazione   di   cuore."
when   one   suffers   of asthma   and   of   palpitation   of   (the) heart

"La   siora   Nina   era   in   una   continua   trepidazione   davanti
The   lady   Nina   was   in   a   continues   trepidation   before

a   un   *omo*   *de*   *tanto*   *riguardo*,   molto   più   che   Malgoni,
to   a   *man*   *of*   *so much*   *esteem*   a lot   more   that   Malgoni
()   *(uomo)*   (there)

indulgente   su   molte   cose,   diventava   ancor   il   *paron*
indulgent   on   many   things   became   still   the   *master*
                                                            (again)   *(padrone)*

terribile,   quando   si   trattava   d'invitare   a   pranzo   l'illustre
terrible   when   itself   dealt   to invite   to   lunch   the illustrious
                                    (happened)

Franzon.   Guai   se   il   manzo   non   era   a   giusta   cottura!
Franzon   Troubles   if   the   beef   not   was   at   correct   cooking

guai   se   il   caffè   non   aveva   quel   tal   profumo   delicato!"
troubles   if   the   coffee   not   had   that   such   scent   delicate

"Guai   se   Nina   non   faceva   gl'inchini   bene   e   non
Troubles   if   Nina   not   made   the curtseys   well   and   not
(It was bad)

rispondeva   a   tono: 'Sior   sì,   sor   dottor;   sior   no,   sor
(she) answered   to   tone   Sir   yes   mr   doctor   sir   no   mr

professor... '"
professor

"Un   omo   che   aveva   delle   influenze   a   Corte,   che,   con
A   man   that   had   of the   influences   at   (the) Court   that   with
   (uomo)   (who)   ()

poco   rispetto   parlando,   aveva   visto   un'arciduchessa   in
little   respect   speaking   had   seen   an archduchess   in
         (about)

camicia,   un   dottor   di   quella   forza,   un   professoron   come
shirt   a   doctor   of   that   power   a   great professor   like

Franzon,   che   si   degna   de   magnar   la   tua   minestra,
Franzon   that   himself   deigned   to   eat   the   your   soup
                  (mangiare)   ()

non   è   un   caso   che   cápita   a   tutti;   oltre   all'onore,
not   (it) is   a   case   that   happens   to   all   beyond   (to) the honor

poteva   sempre   far   del   bene   a   un   imperiale   e   regio
(it) could   always   make   (of)   well   to   an   imperial   and   regal
         (do)   (good)

impiegato,   onesto,   religioso   e   di   sani   principii."
employee   honest   religious   and   of   healthy   principles

"Ho   capito.   La   siora   Nina   non   si   divertiva   troppo."
(I) have   understood   The   lady   Nina   not   herself amused   too much

"E   no,   poverina!   quando   i   due   cravattoni   cominciavano
And   no   little poor one   when   the two   big ties (shots)   began

a   parlar   di   politica,   e   a   tirare   in   scena   la   Dieta   e
to   speak   of   politics   and to   to pull   in   scene   the   Regime (of Hungary)   and

Metternich   e   a   parlare   in   *barlich*   e   *barloch*   e   in   *flit*
Metternich (statesman for the Austrian Empire)   and to   speak   in   *barlich* (fake german)   and   *barloch* (fake german , etc)   and   in   *flit*

e   *futter*,   essa   usciva   volentieri   col   secchiello   a   prender
and   *futter*   she   exited   willing (gladly)   with the   bucket   to   take

l'acqua   sul   pianerottolo.   Era   in   quei   momenti   e   durante
the water   to the   landing   (It) was   in   those   moments   and   during

quelle   brevi   scappate   ch'io   coglievo   l'occasione   per
those   short   escapes   that I   picked   the occasion   for

recitarle   il   mio   sonettino."
to recite her   (the)   mine   little sonnet

"Per dirle che le volevo bene, per baciarle la punta
For to say her that her (I) wanted well for to kiss her the tip

di un dito. Non più in là, s'intende."
of a finger Not more in here itself means (of course)

"Essa non era donna da dar confidenze agli studenti
That one not (she) was woman for to give confidence to students (intimacy)

e io, povero matricolino, ero troppo ingenuo per far
and I poor registered (freshman) (I) was too ingenuous for to make (be)

della concorrenza a Metternich."
(of) competition to Metternich

"La cosa andò avanti così un bel pezzo, tra un trillo
The thing went ahead therefore a nice piece between a trill (while)

di flauto, un sonetto e un secchiello d'acqua, quando
of flute a sonnet and a bucket of water when (the)

Malgoni ammalò gravemente di quel suo battito di
Malgoni became ill seriously of that his beating of

cuore e parve sul punto d'andarsene all'altro mondo."
(the) heart and seemed on point to go himself there to the other world

"Franzon si mise al letto dell'amico e gli usò una
Franzon himself set at the bed of the friend and him was of use as an

assistenza fraterna."
attendance brotherly

"Quando non bastava il dì, rimaneva la notte accanto
When not (it) was enough the day (he) remained the night next

alla siora Nina che scaldava i brodi; e siccome ogni
to mrs Nina that warmed the soups and since every

servizio merita compenso, e non c'è amicizia che in
service deserves compensation and not there is friendship that in

qualche modo non si faccia pagare, il bravo dottor e
some way not itself makes pay the good doctor and

professor, forte dell'amicizia di Metternich e della sua
professor empowered of the friendship of Metternich and of the its
(of)

prepotenza, credette d'onorare anche la moglie del suo
overbearing believed to honor also the wife of the his
(of)

vecchio amico."
old friend

"La   Nina,   una   povera   servetta   senza   esperienza,   còlta
The   Nina   a   poor   servant girl   without   experience   caught

di   sorpresa,   nella   sua   suggezione,   nella   sua   paura,   al
of   surprise   in the (in)   his   subservience   in the   her   fear   of the

buio,   di   notte,   accanto   al   marito   quasi   morente,
dark   of   (the) night   next   to the   husband   almost   dying

dominata   dalla   forza   d'una   passione   brutale   e   poi
dominated   by the   force   of a   passion   brutal   and   then

spaventata   dal   sofisma   del   fallo   compiuto,   dopo   essere
scared   from the   false reasoning   of the   deed   completed   after   to be (have)

stata   vittima,   si   credette   quasi   complice   del   tradimento.
been   victim   herself   believed   nearly   accomplice   of the   treason

E   tacque   e   simulò."
And   (she) kept silent   and   simulated

"Franzon   poteva   fare   del   bene   a   Malgoni;   ma   poteva
Franzon   could   do   of the ()   good   to   Malgoni   but   (he) could

anche   fargli   del   male."
also   do him   of the ()   bad

"La   povera   donna,   sprovveduta   nella   sua   ingenua
The   poor   woman   unprovided   in the   her   ingenuous
                                                            (in)

ignoranza   d'ogni   energia   morale,   credette,   simulando,   di
ignorance   of every   energy   moral   believed   simulating   of

evitare   a   suo   marito   un   gran   dolore.   C'era   da   farlo
to avoid   to   her   husband   a   large   pain   It was   from   make him
                                                                              [to make   him]

morire   di   crepacuore   quel   pover'uomo,   se   gli   avesse
die   of   heartache   that   poor man   if   him   had
                                                                        (was)

detto   di   qual   refe   era   fatta   l'amicizia   di   Franzon."
said   of   what   thread   was   made   the friendship   of   Franzon

"E   non   si   accorse   che   intanto   l'uomo   scaltro   ed
And   not   himself   noticed   that   while   the man   wily   and
         ()

erudito   la   dominava   con   la   sua   stessa   paura   e
erudite   her   dominated   with   the   her   own   fear   and
                                          ()

l'appoggiava   come   una   schiava   al   carro   della   sua
her supported   like   a   slave   to the   wagon   of the   her
                                                                  (of)

colpa."
guilt

"Quando tornai a Padova, dopo le vacanze, mi parve
When (I) returned to Padova after the vacations me (it) seemed

di leggere nel volto meno chiaro della bella Nina
of to read in the face less clear of the beautiful Nina
()

come una nota misteriosa di dolore e di avvilimento.
like a note mysterious of pain and of disheartenment

Essa mi fece capire che aveva qualche ragione
It me made understand that (she) had some reason

segreta di vivi dispiaceri."
secret of lively displeasures

"Malgoni stava abbastanza bene e aveva ripigliato il
Malgoni was enough well and had picked up again the
()

suo ufficio; ma l'amico di casa s'era impadronito così
his office but the friend of (the) house himself was gotten hold so
(had)

bene del cuore del suo malato, che ormai il pover'
well of the heart of the its sick that by now the poor
(of)

uomo non vedeva che per gli occhi del dottore, non
man not saw that for the eyes of the doctor not
(by)

parlava che per la sua bocca."
(he) spoke that by the his mouth
(the same as) ()

"Non ci vuole che un marito per non vedere: ma la
Not us wants that a husband for not to see but the
(but)

gente cominciò a mormorare."
people began to whisper

"Le donnette volevan quasi far credere che il dottore
The little wives wanted almost to make believe that the doctor

mirasse ad avvelenare Malgoni colla digitale o a
aimed to poison Malgoni with the fingers or to

corroderne la vita coi deprimenti. Questa calunnia,
corrode of him the life with the depressings This slander

messa fuori colla solita sventatezza delle teste piccine,
put outside with the usual airheadedness of the heads small
(forth) (stupidity)

non fu senza conseguenza per una fantasia riscaldata
not was without consequence for an imagination heated
(hot)

come la mia; la malinconia, il pallore e le lagrime
like the mine the melancholy the pallor and the tears
()

della povera siora Nina non erano per se un terribile
of the poor mrs Nina not were by themselvesa a terrible
(they)

capo d'accusa?"
head of accusation
(case)

"Da quel dì cominciai a guardare in cagnesco il
From that day (I) began to watch in suspicion the
(with)

piccolo dottor Grobian, dal naso d'aquilotto, dalle spalle
small doctor Grobian, from the nose of eaglet from the shoulders
(with the) (of an eaglet) (with the)

di facchino, che andava schiacciato sotto l'enorme tuba
of (a) porter that went crushed under the enormous tuba

e infagottato nell'enorme cravattone di seta."
and bundled in the enormous scarf of silk

"E siccome ringhio suscita ringhio, anche Franzon
And as snarling provokes snarling also Franzon

imparò a conoscermi e a guardarmi in cagnesco tutte
learned to know me and to look at me in suspicion all

le volte che m'incontrava sul pianerottolo o nell'androne
the times that me met on the landing or in the entrance hall
(he met me)

della casa. Anche lui aveva le sue spie, e qualcuno
of the house Also he had the his spies, and someone
()

doveva avergli parlato dei miei sonetti e de' miei trilli
must have him spoken of the my sonetti and of my melodies

di flauto."
of (the) flute

"Si   arrestava   con   sfacciaggine   a   squadrarmi,   colle
Himself (He) halted   with   brazenness   to   frame me   with the
()   (look well at me)

mani   dietro   alla   schiena,   colle   quali   dimenava   una
hands   behind   to the   back   with the   which   (he) wagged   a

grossa   canna   come   una   coda   e   con   quegli   occhi
large   stick   like   a   tail   and   with   those   eyes

pesti   pareva   dirmi: 'Ocio',   matricolino   che   so   tutto   e   ti
pesky   seemed   to tell me Be careful   registered   that   (I) know all   and   you
                                                (student)

posso   far   legare."
can   make   tie

"Il   *Trovatore*,   aveva   delle   velleità   patriottiche   io   era
The   *Trovatore*   had   of the   ambition   patriotic   I   was
         (Finder)

allora   un   bel   giovinotto,   con   un   bel   pizzo   di   barba: e
then   a   handsome young man   with   a   good   point   of   (the) beard and

anche   quel   po'   di   barba   poteva   essere   interpretata
also   that   little   of   beard   could   be   interpreted
                               ()

come   un'idea   sovversiva.   Parlo   dei   tempi   dei   tedeschi."
as   an idea   subversive   (I) speak of the   times   of the   Germans

"Messo tra un marito geloso e un ringhioso amico di
Put between a husband jealous and a growling friend of

casa, il meno che potessi fare era di usar prudenza,
(the) house the less that you could do was of to use precaution

di rimettere il flauto nell'astuccio, di sacrificare qualche
of to put back the flute in the sheath of to sacrifice some

sonetto, di compatire da lontano a una povera donna
sonnets of to pity from afar to a poor woman
()

caduta come un'agnella negli unghioni d'un orso buono
fallen like a lamb in the claws of a bear good

e stupido e di un lupo furbo e affamato. E le cose
and stupid and of a wolf clever and starved And the things

sarebbero andate avanti un pezzo così, e sarebbero
would be gone ahead a bit like this and would be
(would have) (would have)

fors'anche finite in qualche maniera colla pace e colla
maybe also ended in some way with the peace and the

noia, se tutto ad un tratto l'illustre Franzon non fosse
boredom if all at a strike the illustrious Franzon not was
[all of a sudden] (had)

stato ufficiato ad assumere la direzione dell'Ospedale
been named to assume the direction of the Hospital

delle partorienti a Venezia."
of the women in labour at Venice
(in)

"Carica che portava il grado di medico di Corte e il titolo di cavalier della Corona di ferro. Bagatella!"

"Questa nomina che lusingava la sfrenata ambizione e l'avidità del bravo ginecologo, poteva essere per la siora Nina una vera liberazione. Ma la poverina aveva fatto i conti senza il lupo. Franzon non era un uomo da rinunciare troppo facilmente a una passione e a una comodità, neanche per l'onore della Corona di ferro."

"Scrisse da Venezia all'amico che c'era una bella
(He) wrote from Venice to the friend that there was a beautiful

combinazione, un posto vacante alla contabilità di quella
combination a place vacant to the accounting of that (some)

delegazione, con qualche vantaggio di soldo, che lui
delegation with some advantage of money that he

poteva raccomandarlo a persone influenti."
could recommend him to persons influential

"E poi tornò a scrivere che l'aria delle lagune più
And then (he) returned to write that the air of the lagoons more
(continued)

calma, più carica di sale, era fatta apposta per i
calm more loaded of salts was made on purpose for the

mancamenti di respiro; non perdessero tempo, inoltrassero
sufferings of breathing not lose time forward
(don't)

subito una domanda all'I. R. delegato: al resto pensava
immediately a request to the I . R . delegated to the rest thought
[Imperial Regal] (of the) (would think)

lui..."
he

"Il lupo voleva avere la pecorella vicina..."
The Wolf wanted to have the little sheep close

"Precisamente così. La povera Nina che di quella
Precisely so The poor Nina that of that

maledizione ne aveva abbastanza, usò di tutta la sua
curse of it had enough used of () all the () her

influenza presso il marito perchè non si movesse; gli
influence near the husband why not himself (he) moved () (should move) him

dimostrò che a Padova stavan bene, che vi avevano
(she) demonstrated that at Padova were well [they were fine] that there (they) had

amici e parenti, una bella casa, tutte le migliori
friends and relatives a beautiful house all the better

comodità, mentre un trasloco è una tempesta, un
comfort while a move is a storm a

danno, un fastidio infinito.
curse an annoyance infinite

"Pregò tanto, carezzò tanto la barba grigia del suo
(She) Prayed   so much   caressed   so much   the   beard   grey   of the   her

Malgoni, che costui, pigro già la sua parte e nemico
Malgoni   that   that one   lazy   already   the   his   part   and   enemy
(for)

dei trambusti, finì col ringraziare l'amico lontano e disse
of   bustles   ended   with the   thanking   the friend   far away   and   (he) said

di no."
of   no
()

"Questa risposta non fece che aguzzare la voglia
This   answer   not   made   that   to sharpen   the   wish
(anything but)

dell'illustre ginecologo e colla voglia il dispetto e la
of the illustrious   gynecologist   and   with the   wish   the   spite   and   the

rabbia. Tornò a scrivere; ma vedendo che sprecava il
anger   (He) returned   to   write   but   seeing   that   (he) wasted   the
(repeated)   ()

suo inchiostro, e che Malgoni era deciso a non
his   ink   and   that   Malgoni   was   decided   to   not

muoversi, cominciò a insinuare bel bello qualche
move   (he) began   to   insinuate   beautiful   beautiful   some
[here ,   with nice words]

sospetto nell'animo dell'amico."
suspicion   in the mind   of the friend

"Gli fece capire che la Nina aveva qualche motivo di
Him (he) made understand that the Nina had some reason of
()

non abbandonar Padova, città allegra, piena di studenti
not to abandon Padova city glad full of students

e di capi scarichi, che fanno all'amore coi sonettini e
and of heads drained that make to with the sonnets and
(who) () the () love (with)

coi trilli di flauto..."
with the melodies of (the) flute
(with)

"Birbo!"
Rascal

"... Tre volte birbo! Il marito, facile a insospettirsi, aprì
Three times rascal The husband easy to become suspicious opened

gli occhi, osservò dissimulò, e può essere che
the eyes observed disguised and (it) can be that

cogliesse qualche segno a volo."
(he) picked some sign to flight

"Ma non volendo far scene per paura d'uno scandalo,
But not wanting to make scenes for fear of a scandal

una sera, detto fatto, annuncia alla Nina che aveva
one evening said fact (he) announces to the Nina that (he) had
[as a (he) (to)
completed fact]

accettato il posto: si preparasse a sbarazzare la casa
accepted the post himself prepared to get rid of the house
(position)

e a partire per Venezia, La povera donna, che
and to leave for Venice, The poor woman, that

cominciava appena a respirare e a godere la sua
began just to breathe and to enjoy the her
()

libertà, còlta in un momento cattivo, dichiarò a Malgoni
freedom caught in a moment bad declared to Malgoni

che lei a Venezia non sarebbe andata..."
that she at Venice not would be gone

"'Ah! tu non vuoi venire?' , gridò con voce ironica il
Ah you not want to come screamed with voice ironical the

vecchio geloso:"
old jealous
(man)

"E   siccome   l'amico   lontano   in   quei   giorni   aveva   avuta
And   as   the friend far away   in   those   days   had   had

la   bontà   d'inviargli   tutta   la   raccolta   de'   miei   sonetti
the   goodness of to send him all   the   collection   of   my   sonnets

innocenti,   in   cui   il   nome   di   *Nina*   tornava   spesso   a
innocent   in   which the   name   of   *Nina*   returned   often   to

rimare   con   *divina*,   armato   di   quei   documenti,   si   scagliò
rhyme   with   *divine*   armed   of   those   documents   himself threw

sulla   povera   donna   e   cominciò   a   batterla."
on the   poor   woman   and began   to   strike her

"'So   tutto,   svergognata!   so   tutto,   brutta   traditora,   senza
(I) know all   shameless   (I) know all   ugly   traitor   without
                    (shameless woman)

cuore   e   senza   carità.   E   tu   fai   all'amore,   mentre   hai
heart   and without charity   And you   make   to the love   while   have
                                                    (love)   (you have)

il   marito   malato,   quasi   moribondo?'"
the   husband   sick   nearly   dying

"'E tu dimentichi così il bene che ti ho fatto, brutta
And you forget thus the good that you (I) have done ugly

servaccia?'"
stupid servant

"E siccome non cessava di picchiare con un pezzo di
And since not (he) stopped of to beat with a piece of
()

riga sulla spalla e sulla testa della povera donna, alle
line on the back and on the head of the poor woman, to the

grida, ai pianti di costei, sì risvegliò la casa, si aprì
screams to the cries of that one yes (she) woke up the house itself opened
(were)

qualche finestra, comparvero dei lumi e cominciarono gli
some window appeared of the lights and began the
()

uhè.... di sotto e di sopra. La Nina che non capiva
hey from under and from above The Nina that not understood
()

bene per colpa di chi la battesse il suo padrone,
well for guilt of who her struck the her master

aveva cercato di scappare dall'uscio sul ballatoio;"
had tried of to escape from the exit on the gallery

"E fu allora che il vecchio esasperato, pensando che
And (it) was then that the old exasperated, thinking that
(exasperated man)

volesse fuggire di casa, le sbarrò il passo, l'afferrò
(she) wanted to escape from (the) house her blocked the way her seized

pei capelli e la fece strillare come un'aquila."
by the hairs and her made scream like an eagle
(hair)

"Era troppo ormai anche per un matricolino. Corsi di
(That) Was too much by now also for a registered (I) ran from
(student)

sopra, piombai su quel disperato, che al mio comparire
above fell on that deprived that at the my appearance
(deprived man) (at)

si fece livido; poi non so dire quel che sia avvenuto.
himself made livid then not (I) know to say which that would be happened
(would have)

Pare che l'emozione fosse troppo forte per il vecchio
(It) Seems that the emotion was too strong for the old

malaticcio, o che una violenta stretta di cuore
sick or that a violent tightening of (the) heart
(sick man)

soffocasse insieme la bile, il sangue e la vita."
choked together the bile the blood and the life

"Cadde come un sacco slegato, lo circondarono, lo
(He) Fell / like / a / bag / untied / him / (they) encircled / him

portarono sul letto, e nella notte stessa morì, con
(they) carried / on the bed / and / in the / night / same / (he) died / with

infinito spavento della povera Nina, che s'immaginava
infinite / fright / of the / poor / Nina / that / herself imagined

quasi d'averlo ammazzato."
nearly / of to have him killed

"Due giorni dopo questi fatti alcuni compagni corsero a
Two / days / after / these / facts / some / companions / ran / to

casa mia ad avvertirmi che avevano arrestato Branchetti,
house / mine / to / warn me / that / (they) had / arrested / Branchetti

il direttore del *Trovatore* e che la polizia era in cerca
the / director / of the / *Trovatore* / and / that / the / police / was / in / search

di me. Non era il caso di stare ad aspettarla."
of / me / Not / was / the / case / of / to stand / to / wait for it
/ / / (it was) / (time)

"Le guardie entrarono in casa mia e sequestrarono le
The guards entered in house mine and seized the

carte, le robe, il flauto."
papers the clothes the flute

"Padova non era più aria buona per me: e per non
Padua not was (any)more air good for me and for not
(healthy)

aspettare di peggio, la notte stessa presi la strada del
to wait for of worse the night same (I) took the road of the

confine."
border

"Era anche questo un intrigo di Franzon?"
Was also this an intrigue of Franzon

"... Còlto nel segno!"
Caught in the sign
(Visible) (signature)

"Coll'ingegno che natura gli ha dato, egli aveva saputo
With the talent that nature him has given he had known

dimostrare alla polizia centrale di Venezia che a
to demonstrate to the police central of Venice that at

Padova si congiurava contro l'ordine costituito e che un
Padua (they) schemed against the order institutional and that a

branco di giovinastri mazziniani nelle conventicole del
gang of giovinastri mazzinians in the clique of the
(mazziniani; followers of Guiseppe Mazzini; Italian republican)

Trovatore inneggiavano all'Italia sotto l'allegorico nome di
Trovatore sang praise to the Italy under the allegorical name of

Nina;"
Nina

"Che talento! Non poteva vendicarsi con più spirito. E
That talent Not (he) could take revenge with more spirit And

come finì?"
how ended
(ended it)

"Finì　che,　morto　Malgoni　e　venuto　al　mondo,　sei　mesi
(It) Ended　that　died　Malgoni　and　came　to the　world　six　months

dopo　il　funerale,　un　bel　maschietto,　la　povera　Nina
after　the　funeral　a　beautiful　male boy　the　poor　Nina

trovò　ancora　della　sua　convenienza　di　andare　a
found　still　of the (to)　her　convenience　of　to go ()　to

Venezia　e　d'acconciarsi　in　casa　del　suo　nuovo　padrone
Venice　and　of to set up herself　in　(the) house　of the (of)　her　new　master

e　tiranno;　il　quale　qualche　tempo　dopo　trovò　della
and　tyrant　the　which　some　time　after　found　of the (to)

sua　convenienza　anche　lui　di　sposare　la　vedova　e
his　convenience　also　him　of　to marry　the　widow　and

tirarsi　in　casa　quel　po'　di　ben　di　Dio　che　Malgoni
to pull himself in　house　that　bit　of　good (goods)　of　God　that　Malgoni

le　aveva　lasciato　sul　testamento.　La　siora　Nina
her　had　left　on the (in the)　testament　The　mrs　Nina

dev'essere　morta　qualche　tempo　prima　che　entrassero
must be (must have)　died　some　time　before　that　entered

gli　Italiani　in　Venezia."
the　Italians　in　Venice

"Bella　storia!　e　Franzon?"
Beautiful　story　and　Franzon

"Franzon sano, robusto, vispo come un pesce, di
Franzon healthy sturdy lively as a fish from

trionfo in trionfo, oggi è diventato una mezza
triumph in triumph today is become an average
(has)

illustrazione della scienza europea. Si dice che alla
illustration of the science European One says that to the

prima infornata abbiano a farlo senatore."
first oven batch (they) have to make him senator
(meeting)

"... È naturale! Non son più i tempi dei tedeschi."
Is natural Not (they) are (any) more the times of the Germans
(That's) (logical)

DUE SPOSI IN VIAGGIO
TWO SPOUSES IN (A) JOURNEY
(ON)

La giornata spuntò serena e limpida per gli sposi, che
The day appeared serene and limpid for the spouses that

dopo aver riposato una notte a Como, continuarono il
after to have rested one night at Como, continued the ()

loro viaggio verso la Tremezzina. L'acquazzone del
their journey towards the Tremezzina The heavy rain of the
(Tremezzina; community in Northern Italy on lake Como)

giorno prima aveva posto nell'aria i brividi precursori
day before had placed in the air the chills precursory

del non lontano ottobre e le cime dei monti, e
of the not far away October and the tops of the mounts, and

specialmente delle Alpi, brizzolate di neve, splendevano
especially of the Alps speckled of snow shone
(with)

sotto un raggio alquanto diluito e raffreddato
under a beam somewhat diluted and cooled

nell'atmosfera trasparente.
in the atmosphere clear

Qualche giogo più acuminato usciva dalle altre vette, in
Some   ridge more sharp   exited from the other summits in

un vestito roseo,   allegro come quello d'una fanciulletta
a   dress   rose-colored merry   like that   of a   little girl

il   giorno di Pasqua,   sotto un cielo chiaro   chiaro; e
the day   of Passover   under a   sky   clear   clear   and
                                              [very clear   ]

scendendo   a   poco   a   poco   lungo la   schiena dei   monti,
coming down to   little   by   little along the back   of the mountains
             [slowly   ]

dopo   il   verde giallo dei   pascoli   rasi, vedevi   il   verde
after the green yellow of the pastures mowed (you) saw the green

bruno dei   castani,   poi   sterratelli   bianchi di campi
brown of the chestnuts then small excavations white   of fields
                                (sterrato; excavation; elli (diminutive plural))

seminati a   saraceno,   poi   ancora i   colori vivaci dei
seeded   to   buckwheat   then also   the colors lively of the
          (with)

giardini e   il   bianco delle   villette,   che   scappavano
gardens   and the white   of the little villas that escaped
                                                         (passed)

innanzi al   battello,   dolci dolci, come le   cartine   in un
before   to the little boat sweet sweet   as   the pictures in a

organetto   a   manubrio.
little organ by handle

Bastiano, lo sposo, stando in piedi, osservava queste
Bastiano   spouse   being   in   feet   observed   these
     [standing up]

meraviglie con un cannocchiale da teatro, che si era
wonders   with   a   binocular   from   theatre   that   himself was
     ()   (binoculars)   (had)

fatto prestare da qualcuno, e quando una folata d'aria
made   loan   from   someone   and   when   a   gust   of air
           (of wind)

l'investiva più fortemente, di sotto alle lenti, incartocciava
him assailed   more   strongly   of   under   to the   lenzes   papered
           (crumpled up)

la faccia, socchiudeva gli occhi, con quella espressione
the   face   closed   the   eyes   with   that   expression

dolorosa, che hanno certe slavate sindoni d'altare di
painful   that   have   certain   washed out   shrouds   of altar   of

campagna.
(the) countryside

Si era anche abbottonato il suo bel soprabito d'autunno
Himself was   also   buttoned up   the   his   nice   overcoat   of autumn
()   (Had)   ()

color d'uva passa, tutto fino al bavero.
color   of grape   passed   wholly   until   to the   collar
       (up)

Ma   di   sotto,   la   valigietta   dei   denari,   posta   a   tracolla,
But   of   under   the   little wallet   of the   money   placed   at   (the) shoulder
[under it]

e   in   croce   a   questa   l'astuccio   del   cannocchiale,
and   in   cross   to   this   the sheath   of the   telescope

cadendo   sui   due   fianchi,   facevano   un   rigonfiamento   in
falling   on the   two   flanks   made   a   swelling   in

fondo   alla   schiena,   che   dava   delle   arie   d'inglese   al
bottom   to the   back   that   gave   of the   airs   of Englishman   to the

signor   Bastiano   Malignoni   di   Monza.
Mr .   Bastiano   Malignoni   of   Monza

Nel   passare   sul   battello   dimenticò   d'essere   un   uomo
In the   passing   on the   boat   (he) forgot   of to be   a   man

alto   e   urtò   il   suo   cappello   nuovo,   incatramato,   d'un
tall   and   hit   the   his   hat   new   tarred   of a
()   (blackened)

bel   taglio   tutto   monzese,   contro   un   voltino,   facendovi
beautiful   cut   all   monzese   against   a   little roof   making there

dentro   un'ammaccatura   a   triangolo,   che   egli   portava,
in   a dent   to   triangle   that   he   carried
[triangle formed]

senza   saperlo,   con   una   certa   dignità.
without   to know it   with   a   sure   dignity

Prima ancora d'arrivare a Torno, ebbe un battibecco col
Before yet to arrive at Torno (he) had a squabble with the

revisore dei biglietti, perchè gli sposi avevano in fallo
controller of the tickets because the spouses had in (by) mistake

occupati i primi posti coi biglietti dei secondi:
occupied the first places with the tickets of the second

Fatto sta che il signor Bastiano dovette in faccia a
Fact was that the Mr. Bastiano had to in face (view) to (of)

tutti i signori e a tutte le signore inglesi pagare una
all the gentlemen and to all the ladies English to pay a

differenza, arrossendo fino alle orecchie, come s'egli
difference blushing until (up) to the ears like himself he

avesse avuto intenzione di non dare a Cesare quel
would have had (the) intention of not to give to Caesar that

ch'è di Cesare.
which is of Caesar

Spiegò poi l'abbaglio a Paolina, dimostrandole come sui
(He) Explained then the blunder to Paolina demonstrating her how on the

bastimenti *d'acqua* quel che è primo per i vagoni di
ships of water that one that is first for the wagons of

terra diventa ultimo, e quel che ivi è ultimo qui
land becomes last and that one that there is last here

diventa primo, precisamente come vedremo nella valle di
becomes first just like (we) will see in the valley of

Josafat, il giorno del giudizio universale.
Josafat the day of the judgment universal
[the last judgement]

Paolina, la sposa, stava zitta, come se non gliene
Paolina the spouse was silent as if not her it

importasse, e continuava a girare sopra sè stessa in
imported and continued to turn over herself self in

contemplazione di tutto lo spettacolo che aveva intorno,
contemplation of all the spectacle that (she) had around

voltando per caso un poco di spalle al marito.
turning by case a little of shoulders to the husband
[coincidentally] [with the back]

Essa	vestiva	un	abito	povero,	povero,	color	ferro
She	wore	a	dress	poor	poor	color	iron
				[very poor	]		

brunito,	ma	la	sposa	di	provincia	la	si	conosceva
burnished	but	the	spouse	of	province	her	one	recognised

all'oro	giallo	della	sua	guarnizione,	al	cappellino	col
at the gold	yellow	of	her	trimming	at the	little hat	with the

pettirosso	schiacciato	in	un	angolo,	cinto	da	una	gran
robin	crushed	in	a	corner	encircled	by	a	large

veletta	celeste,	che	svolazzava,	stridendo	e	folleggiando
veil	celestial	that	flapped	screaming	and	clashing

sulla	testa,	sulle	guancie,	pallide,	e	sul	collo,	con
on the	head	on the (with)	cheeks	pale	and	on the (the)	neck	with

vibrazioni	serpentine.
vibrations	snake-like

Il	sole	dopo	uno	svolto,	la	investì	in	un	momento
The	sun	after	a	turn	her	invested	in	a	moment

che	Bastiano	risaliva	il	ponte.
that	Bastiano	returned onto	the	bridge

Talchè,   in   vederla,   gli   parve   che   al   luccicar   delle   gioie
Such that   in   to see her   him   (it) seemed   that   by the   sparkling   of the   jewels

e   al   contrasto   del   sole   sulla   veletta,   ella   si
and   by the   contrast   of   sun   on the   veil   she   herself

accendesse   come   una   fiamma   di   spirito   di   vino.   Gli
ignited   like   a   flame   of   alcohol   of   wine   Him

parve   anche   di   essere   alto   come   il   monte   Bisbino,
(it) seemed   also   of   to be   high   like   the   mount   Bisbino

che   stavano   girando,   e   che   non   bastasse   ancora   a
that   (they) were   turning around   and   that   not   (it) was enough   still   to

contenere   tutta   la   sua   felicità.
contain   all   the   his   happiness

Paolina   era   la   prima   in   trentasei   anni   di   vita   che   egli
Paolina   was   the   first   in   thirtysix   years   of   life   that   he

aveva   amato,   o   almeno   la   prima,   sulla   quale   avesse
had   loved   or   at least   the   first   on the   which   (he) had

voluto   fondare   un   pensiero   con   qualche   conclusione.
wanted   to base   a   thought   with   some   conclusion

E a vedersela ora davanti, a due passi, "bella come
And to see himself her now before at two steps beautiful as

una rosa" il signor Malignoni non invidiava nessuno
a rose the Mr. Malignoni not envied nobody
( )

de'suoi vicini, nemmeno quell'inglese o americano, che
of his neighbors not even that English or American that

da una mezz'ora andava contando monete d'oro e
since one half hour went counting coins of gold and

d'argento.
of silver

"Sei contenta?"
Are satisfied
(you)

"Sì, un po' freddo."
Yes a bit cold

E si stringeva in uno scialle scozzese, come se
And herself tightly wound in a scarf Scottish as if

volesse farsi poca e sparire.
(she) wanted to make herself small and to disappear

"Hai   fame?"
(You) Have hunger

"Nulla."
None

"Io   ho   fame."
I   have   hunger

"Io   no."
I   not

"Vuoi   che   andiamo   nella   sala   di   sotto?"
(You) Want that   (we) go   in the   room   of   below

"No,   stiamo   qui."
Not   (we) stay   here

108 Due Sposi in Viaggio

"È   bello,   non   è   vero   che   è   bello?"
Is   beautiful not   is   true   that   is   beautiful
(It is)   (is it)   (it is)

"Sì,   molto."
Yes   very

"Vuoi   un   caffè   o   una   tazza   di   birra?"
(You) Want a   coffee   or   a   cup   of   beer

"Ti   pare?   Sto   bene."
You   seems   I'm   well
[Does it seem to you that I would?]

Tornavano   a   tacere   per   un   pezzo.
Returned   to   be silent   for   a   piece
(They returned)   (while)

Quelle   rive   strette   fra   l'acqua   e   il   verde   dei   monti,
Those   rivers tightened between the water and the green   of the mountains

quel   succedersi   di   colori   dai   più   chiassosi   ai   più
those   to succeed itself of   colors   from   more   rowdy   to   more

delicati,   dal vino   al latte,   da   una   villetta   di   zucchero
delicate   from the wine   to the milk from a   little villa   of   sugar

a   una   incassatura   rocciosa   e   tosta,   irta   di   punte;   quel
to   a   inbedding   rocky   and burned   full   of   spikes   that

succedersi   di   artifici   per   andare   a   godere   una   spanna
succeeding itself   of   tricks   for   to go   to   enjoy   a   span

di   sasso,   una   bricca,   un   pratello   largo   come   un
of   stone   a   hilltop   a   meadow   wide   as   a

fazzoletto,   quell'aprirsi   sfacciato   di   nuovi   immensi   bacini
handkerchief   that to open itself   brazen   of   new   immense   basins

d'acqua,   pieni   di   azzurro   e   di   luce,   là   dove   pareva
of water   full   of   blue   and of   light   there   where   (it) seemed

che   fosse   tutto   finito;   e   il   chiacchierare   della   gente   ad
that   (it) was   all   ended   and the   chatting   of the   people   at
       (had)

ogni   stazione   fra il   battello   e   la   riva,   fra   chi   scende
every   station   between the   boat   and the   river   between   who   descends

e   chi   sale;
and   who   goes up

E   il   tonfo   misurato   delle   ruote;   e   il   suono   della
And   the   splash   measured   of the   wheels   and   the   sound   of the
(regular)

campana   che   ridesta   gli   echi   dei   pascoli,   quello
bell   that   wakes   the   echoes   of the   pastures   that

spettacolo   insomma   mosso   e   chiuso   fra   due   coperchi
spectacle   in short   moved   and   closed   between   two   covers

lucidi   ed   opalini,   l'acqua   e   il   cielo,   occupava   l'anima
polished   and   opal   the water   and   the   sky   occupied   the mind

di   Paolina,   se   pure   non   si   deve   credere   ch'ella
of   Paolina   as   also   not   one   must   believe   that she

facesse   di   tutto   per   occuparsene...
did   of   everything   for   to occupy herself with it
()

La   natura   le   si   dipingeva   innanzi   bella   ed   innocente,
The   nature   her   itself   painted   before   beautiful   and   innocent

ed   essa,   contenta   di   trovarsi   fra   la   gente   e   sotto   il
and   she   happy   of   to find herself   between   the   people   and   under   the

raggio   di   sole,   avrebbe   voluto   che   il   viaggio   non
ray   of   (the) sun   (she) would have   wanted   that   the   journey   not
(rays)

terminasse   più,   che   le   Alpi   si   aprissero   per   dar   luogo
finished   (any)more   that   the   Alps   themselves opened   for   to give   place
(make)   (way)

a   un   altro   lago   sterminato.
to   an   other   lake   extended

Il bacino di Argegno, malinconico più degli altri,
The river basin of Argegno melancholically more of the (than the) others

rispondeva all'ordine dei suoi desiderii e guardando su
answered to the order (to the sort) of the (of) her desires and watching on

ai nudi ceppi delle montagne, alcune delle quali a
to the naked trunks (feet) of the mountains some of which to

picco, alle creste disabitate, a certi andirivieni di luoghi
(the) peak to the crests uninhabited to certain go and come of places

dirupati, si augurava in cuor suo di esservi, non
steep herself (she) wished in heart her of to be there not

importa se perduta, se di notte, o in mezzo alla
was important if (she were) lost if at night or in middle to the

bufera.
storm

Si doveva stare tanto bene in una nicchia, lassù,
One must be so much well in a hollow there-up (up there)

dove mirava un uccellaccio. Vedeva anche qualche
where (she) looked at a poor bird (She) Saw also some

muricciuolo di cimitero...
little wall of (a) cemetary

Il — The
dormire — sleep
lassù — up there
per — for
sempre — always
all'ombra — to the shadow
dei — of
faggi — beeches
e — and
dei — of the

castagni, — chestnut trees
con — with
una — a
povera — poor
croce — cross
sul — over the
capo, — head
anche — also
questo — this

le — him
pareva — seemed
bello — beautiful
in — in
quell'istante — that moment
che — that
il — the
suo () — her
Sebastiano — Sebastiano

l'aveva — her had
lasciata — left
sola — alone
per — for
scendere — to go down
a — to
mangiare — eat
un — a

boccone. — mouthful

Man — Hand
mano — hand (While)
che — that
si — itself
procedeva — proceeded
verso — towards
Bellagio — Bellagio
il — the
battello — boat

si — itself
faceva — made [it became]
sempre — always
più — more
affollato; — crowded
tutti — all
correvano — went
alle — to the
regate. — regattas

Le — The
ville — villas
portavano — carried
la — the
bandiera... — flag

115 Due Sposi in Viaggio

I sandolini dipinti colle signorine dentro tutte a fiori, a
The small boats painted with the young ladies within all to flowers to

nastri, a parasoli bianchi, verdi, rossi, cilestri venivano
ribbons to parasols white green red azure (they) came

in frotta come delfini a prendere l'onda del vapore;
in crowd like dolphins to take the wave of the steamboot

s'intendevano strilli di gioia e campane a festa; il
one understood screams of joy and bells to festivity the
(of)

largo bacino di Menaggio cominciava a spalancarsi in
wide river basin of Menaggio began to open wide itself in

una grande scena scintillante, circonfusa d'una nebbia
a large scene sparkling surrounded of a fog

rosea; si udivano anche gli spari dei mortaretti; poi il
rose-colored one heard also the shootings of fireworks then the

suono delle bande che passavano nelle barche sotto
sound of the bands that passed in the boats under

"gli elmi di Scipio."
the helms of Scipio
(Roman general who defeated Hannibal at Zama; symbol for the Italian unity)

Venivano　acuti　profumi　dalle　serre　e　dagli　spallierati　dei
(There) Came　acute　scents　from the　greenhouses and　from the　stands　of

limoni;　erano　tutti　in　festa,　povera　Paolina!
lemons　they were　all　in　festivity　poor　Paolina

Si　svegliarono　anche　le　dame　inglesi,　anche　le　più
Woke up　also　the　ladies　English　also　the　most

vecchie　in　un　gran　bisbiglio,　sotto　i　grandi　panieri　dei
old　in　a　large　whisper　under　the large　baskets　of the
　　　　　　　　　　　(ing)　　　　　　　　　　　　　　　　()

loro　cappelli　e　segnavano　col　dito　"Belaccio,　Belaccio."
their　hats　and　pointed　with the　finger　Belaccio　Belaccio

Questa　era　la　meta　dei　nostri　sposi.
This　was　the　goal　of the　our　spouses
　　　　　　　　　　(of)

La　gente　cominciò　a　discendere　accalcandosi.
The　people　began　to　come down　crowding eachother

Bastiano stava attento a schivare gli Hôtel, e pregava
Bastiano was careful to evade the Hotel and asked

Paolina di cercare cogli occhi la Trattoria Americana,
Paolina of to try with the eyes the Inn American

dove si mangia bene, il sonno ciascuno se lo porta,
where one eats well the sleep everyone itself there takes

si paga poco e si sta senza soggezione; ma in quel
one pays little and one is without subjection but in that

punto un signore, un vero gentiluomo, pulito e cortese
point a man a true gentleman clean and courteous
(moment)

come un buon padre di famiglia, gli tolse la valigia
like a good father of family him removed the suitcase

di mano.
from (the) hand

"Americana? Americana?" domandò Bastiano.
American American asked Bastiano

"Oui, par ici, monsieur."
Yes through here sir
(*French*)

Il buon signore passò la valigia a un altro signore
The good gentleman passed the suitcase to an other gentleman

coi favoriti biondi, che la buttò sull'imperiale di un
with the whiskers blond that it he threw on the luggage rack of an

omnibus.
omnibus

"Entrez, monsieur, entrez."
Go in sir go in
(*French*)

"Americana?" tornò a domandare Bastiano, sentendosi
American returned to ask Bastiano feeling himself
(repeated)

sospinto come un sacco, e non accorgendosi che col
pushed out like a bag and not noticing that with the

parlare a monosillabi non faceva che ribadire un'opinione
to speak to monosyllables not did but underline an opinion
(speaking) (in) (anything but)

storta nella testa dei due bravi signori.
wrong in the head of the two good gentlemen

Si trovò, prima che potesse orientarsi, insaccato
Himself (he) found before that (he) could orient himself bagged (stuffed)

nell'omnibus fra una dozzina di "yes" lontano sei posti
in the omnibus between a dozen of yes far six places

da Paolina.
from Paolina

In due trotti, ossia cinquanta passi per cavallo,
In two trots that is fifty steps for horse

l'omnibus si fermò innanzi al grand Hôtel Bellagio.
the omnibus itself stopped before to the grand Hotel Bellagio
()

L'albergo era chiuso in giro da una gran cancellata a
The hotel was enclosed in round from a large grate to
[around] (with)

punte d'oro, che serrava un gran giardino all'inglese:
tips of gold that locked a large garden to the English
[English garden]

non c'era scampo, bisognava rassegnarsi.
not there was escape (he) had to submit himself

121 Due Sposi in Viaggio

Alla fin fine il viaggio di nozze non lo si fa che
At the end (of the) end the trip of wedding not it one makes that
(but)

una volta sola.
one time only

Un giovinetto biondo come il lino, in falda nera, colle
A little boy blond like the linen in suit black with the

scarpettine alla francese, pettinato anche lui come uno
little shoes at the French combed also he like a

sposino, li precedette per uno scalone di marmo,
little married man them preceded by a staircase of marble

ornato di statue, di candelabri, di specchi, di acacie,
adorned of statues of branched candlesticks of mirrors of acacias

tintinnando le chiavi e senza mai parlare li condusse
tinkling the keys and without ever to speak them lead

au cinquième fino a una camera che riusciva sopra
to the *fifth* until to a room that opened over
(French)

un cortile stretto, profondo e tetro come un pozzo.
a little courtyard tight deep and dark like a sink

"A onze heures le déjeuner, s'il vous plait", disse
At eleven hours the breakfast if it you pleases (he) said
(*French*)

stando sull'uscio prima di licenziarsi.
standing on the exit before of to relieve himself
(in the door)

"Cosa?" domandò Bastiano, che cominciava a credere
What asked Bastiano who began to believe

d'essere nel mondo della luna.
of being in the world of the moon

"C'est bien", si affrettò a dire Paolina per sbarazzarsene.
It is well herself hurried to say Paolina for to get rid herself of it
(*French*)

I coniugi Malignoni, rimasti soli, si guardarono in faccia
The spouses Malignoni remained alone eachother looked at in face

senza aprir bocca.
without to open mouth

"Ti   avevo   pur   detto   di   stare   attenta   all'Americana."
You   (I) had   also   told   of   to be   careful   to the American
                                 ()

"A   me?   tocca   a   me   di   cercare   l'albergo?"
To   me   touches   to   me   of   to search   the hotel
           [do I have   ]   ()   (to find)

"Così,   oltre   a   pagare   un   occhio   della   testa,   non   si
Therefore   beyond   to   to pay   an   eye   of the   head   not   itself

potrà   veder   nulla,   mangiar   nulla   e   capir   nulla."
will be able   to see   nothing   to eat   nothing   and   to understand   nothing

"Abbiamo   però   una   bella   vista",   disse   con   un
(We) Have   but   a   beautiful   view   said   with   a
           (however)

sogghignerò   sardonico   la   sposina,   ficcando   lo   sguardo
snigger   sardonic   the   spouse   fixing   the   look

nel   fondo   del   cortile.
in the   bottom   of the   courtyard

"Per   me,   scusami,   ma   io   non   ci   sto",   esclamò   lo
For   me   excuse me   but   I   not   here (I) stay   exclaimed   the

sposo.
husband

"Che   vuoi   fare?"
What   (you) want to do

"Vuoi   morire   di   febbre   gialla   o   d'itterizia?"
(You) Want to die   of   fever   yellow   or   of jaundice

"Ebbene,   di'   che   ti   cambino   la   stanza."
Well   tell   that   you   (they) change   the   room

"Non   capiscono   niente: sembra   il   paese   dei   tartari."
Not   (they) understand   nothing   (it) seems   the   country   of the   Tartars

"E   allora   rassegnamoci   fino   a   domattina."
And   then   (we) resign ourselves   until   to   tomorrow morning

"Sai   cosa   faccio?   vado   a   vedere   dov'è   questa   famosa
(You) Know what   (I will) do   (I will) go   to   see   where is   this   famous

Americana,   e   se   il   luogo   è   proprio   come   dicono,
American   and   if   the   place   is   just   like   (they) say

lasciamo   la   valigia   e   pranziamo   là.   Almeno   si   sa
(we) leave   the   suitcase   and   (we) have lunch   there   At least   one   knows

quello   che   si   mangia.   Che   ne   dici?"
that   what   one   eats   What   of it   (you) say

"Io?   nulla."
I   nothing

"No,   devi   dire   anche   il   tuo   parere."
Not   (you) must   to say   also   the   your   opinion

"Che   cosa   devo   dire?"
What   thing   must   say
                 (must I)

"Qualche   cosa."
Some   thing

"Andiamo   a   pranzo   all'Americana."
(We) Go   to   lunch   at the American

"Me   lo   dici   con   tanta   noia."
(To) Me   it   (you) say   with   so much   boredom

"Ti   pare?   Sono   un   po'   stanca."
(To) You (it) seems   (I) Am   a   bit   tired

"Allora,   faccio   così?"
Then   make   therefore

"Sì,   sì."
Yes   yes

"Addio,   angelo."   E   la   carezzò   colla   punta   delle   dita.
To-God   angel   And   her   caressed   with the   tip   of the   fingers
(Goodbye)

"Io   ti   aspetto   qui."
I   you   await   here

"Sì....   e   mi   vuoi   bene?"
Yes   and   me   (you) wish   well

"Che   ragazzo!"
What   (a) boy

"Stella!"
Star

Bastiano uscì. Paolina girò la chiave nella toppa, si
Bastiano exited Paolina turned the key in the hole herself

tolse d'addosso lo scialle, il casacchino, li gettò sul
removed from over the scarf the little over-blouse them threw on the

letto insieme al cappello; chiuse la finestra; si buttò in
bed together to the hat closed the window herself threw in

una poltrona, portò il fazzoletto alla bocca e pianse,
a seat carried the little handkerchief to the mouth and cried

senza lagrime, pianse della gioia di trovarsi sola.
without tears (she) cried of joy of to find herself alone

Bastiano uscì all'aria aperta colle orecchie un po'
Bastiano exited to the air open with the ears a bit

calde. Sotto alla sua grande felicità sentiva una mezza
warm Under to the () his large happiness (he) felt a half

volontà di strozzare qualcuno.
desire of to strangle someone

Passata   però   la   prima   agitazione   e   scoperta   la   sua
Passed   however   the   first   agitation   and   (he) discovered   the   his
()

Americana   sotto   i   portici,   un   buco   fatto   apposta   per
American   under   the   arches   a   hole   made   on purpose   for
(place)

loro,   tornò   tutto   contento   all'albergo   a   trarne   la   sua
them   (he) returned   all   content   to the hotel   to   draw from it   the   his
()

povera   *alma*   *consorte*   che   aveva   lasciata   in   quella
poor   *soul*   *consort*   that   (he) had   left   in   that

muda   lassù.
moult   up there
(fluffy mess)

Quando   gli   sembrò   di   essere   salito   alto   abbastanza,   si
When   him   (it) seemed   of   to be   went up   high   enough   himself

ricordò   di   non   aver   osservato   prima   il   numero   della
(he) remembered   of   not   to have   observed   before   the   number   of the

stanza;   discese   qualche   scala   per   vedere   di   orientarsi
room   (he) descended   some   stairs   for   to see   of   to orient himself

coll'occhio.
with the eye

Infilò   qualche   corridoio   a   destra,   qualche   andito   a
(He) Followed some   corridor   to (the) right   some   little hallway   to

sinistra,   ma   sebbene   non   ci   fosse   dubbio   che   la   scala
(the) left   but   although   not   there was   doubt   that   the   stairs

fosse   quella   stessa,   pure   gli   pareva   di   vedere   qualche
was   the one   same   also   him   (it) seemed   of   to see   some

cosa   di   non   veduto   prima.
thing   of   not   seen   before
          ()

Per   quanto   gli   pesasse,   discese   ad   uno   ad   uno   i
For   how much   him   (it) weighed   (he) descended by   one   to   one   the

gradini,   fino   all'atrio   del   pianterreno,   si   accostò   all'ufficio,
steps   until   to the entrance hall of the   ground floor   himself (he) approached to the office
                                                              ()

dove   stava   scrivendo   un   signore   grasso,   e   domandò
where   was   writing   a   gentleman   fat   and   asked

con   tutta   bella   grazia:
with   all   beautiful grace

"Perdoni,   mi   saprebbe   indicare   dov'è   la   mia   camera?"
Forgive   me   would know   to indicate   where is   the   my   room
                    (would you know)   ()

"Il   numero?"
The   number

"Non   ho   guardato."
Not   (I) have   watched

"La   chiave?"
The   key

"L'ho   lasciata   nell'uscio."
It have   left   in the door
[I have left it]

"Domandi   al   cameriere."
Ask   to the   waiter

"Meno   male!"   pensò   Bastiano.
Less   bad   thought   Bastiano

Questi	almeno	capisce	l'italiano,	e	si	voltò	a	cercare
these	at least	understand	the Italian	and	himself	(he) turned ()	to	search for

quel	biondino	che	l'aveva	condotto	su.	Due	altri
that	blond boy	that	him had	lead	up	Two	other

servitori	o	sopraintendenti	stavano	sulla	porta,	colle	mani
servants	or	overseers	stood	at the	door	with the	hands

sotto	la	coda	dell'abito,	in	atto	di	curiosità	sfaccendata.
under	the	tail	of the coat	in	action	of	curiosity	useless

Bastiano,	non	trovando	il	suo	bel	biondino,	ricominciò
Bastiano	not	finding	the ()	his	handsome	blond	recommenced

da	capo	a	salire	la	scala	colla	speranza	che	hanno
from	head (the beginning)	to	go up	the	stairs	with the	hope	that	have

tutti	gli	scolari,	che	per	andare	in	fine	della	lezione
all	the	scholars	that	for	to go	in	end	of the	lesson

spesso	conviene	ricominciare	da	capo.
often	(it) convenes	to recommence	from	head (the beginning)

Mentre andava su coll'affanno di chi porta un sacco
While (he) went up with the breathlessness of who carries a sack

di sale sulla montagna, vide che i due sopraintendenti
of salt on the mountain (he) saw that the two overseers

l'osservavano, rìdendo sotto il naso.
him observed laughing under the nose

"Questi animali se mi vedessero annegare non mi
These animals if me (they) saw drown not me

darebbero una mano."
(they) would give a hand

Ricordando d'aver inteso uno di quei bravi signori, il
Remembering of to have understood one of those good gentlemen the

più canonico, a parlare il dialetto di Bellagio, che è
more canonical to speak the dialect of Bellagio that is
(natural)

anche quello di Monza, spinse la testa fuori della
also that one of Monza (he) stuck the head outside of the
(over) (the)

ringhiera ed esclamò in dialetto schietto:
railing and exclaimed in dialect blunt

"Vogliono   avere   la   bontà   quei   bravi   signori   d'indicarmi   il
Want   to have the goodness those good   gentlemen to indicate to me the

mio   cameriere,   un   bel   biondino?"
my   chamberboy   a   handsome little blond

"Was?"   domandò   il   tedesco   di   Bellagio,   andando   presso
What   asked   the German   of   Bellagio   going   near
(German)

la   scala   col   viso   rivolto   all'insù   e   le   mani   sotto   la
the stair   with the face turned   to the in up and the hands under the
     (stairs)   (upwards)

coda.
coattail

"Un   giovinotto   magrino..."   tornò   a   dire.
A   young man   very thin   turned to say
                                 (he repeated)

"Was sagen Sie?" ripetè il canonico, mentre il suo
What say you repeated the natural one while the his
(*German*) ()

compare si nascondeva dietro una colonna di marmo
comrade himself hid behind a pillar of marble

per non lasciarsi scorgere a ridere.
for not to let notice to laugh

"Ah gabbiano!" gridò Bastiano, facendo il viso grosso.
Ah gull screamed Bastiano making the face large
(thug)

Il compare dalla colonna scappò in uno stanzino.
The comrade from the pillar escaped in a little chamber

Era una burletta magnifica.
(It) Was a joke magnificent

"Signor   padrone",   seguitò   Bastiano   dall'alto   della   seconda
Mr .   landlord   followed   Bastiano   from the high of the   second

scala   verso   il   bravo   e   gentile   signore   dell'ufficio,   "io
stairs   towards   the   good   and   kind   gentlemen   of the office   I

pago   anch'io   i   miei   bravi   denari   come   tutti   gli   altri,   e
pay   also I   the my   good   money   like   all   the   others   and
                   ()

pretendo   di   essere   servito   come   tutti   gli   altri.   Vogliono
(I) expect of   to be   served   like   all   the   others   (They) Want

accompagnarmi   si   o   no?"
to accompany me yes   or   no

Il   bravo   signore   uscì   dall'ufficio   colla   cannuccia   rossa
The   good   gentleman   exited   from the office   with the   little cane   red
                                                                      (pen)

nell'orecchio   e   rispose:
in the ear   and   answered

"El   xe   inutile   che   facciate   tanto   strepito,   galantomo."
It   is   useless   that   (you) make   so big a   din   brave man
(*dialect*)

"Se   no   gavè   a   memoria   il   numero   de   la   stanza   no
If   not   have   to   memory   the   number   of   the   room   not
                 (dialect)

potemo   tenere   a   mente   tutti   li   numeri..."
(we) can   hold   to   mind   all   the   numbers
            [remember   ]

"Ma   quel   cameriere   che   mi   ha   condotto   prima,   è
But   that   waiter   that   me   has   lead   before   is
                                                                                     (he)

morto   d'accidente,   el   me   caro   galantomo?"   strillò   il
dead   of accident   the   me   beloved   gentleman   yelled   the
                                     (dialect)   ()

signor   ragioniere   Malignoni   di   Monza,   rosso   come   un
Mr .   accountant   Malignoni   of   Monza   red   like   a

gallo,   correndo   abbasso,   presso   quasi   a   perdere   la
rooster   running   down   near   almost   to   lose   the
                                                                      [go mad

tramontana   del   tutto: tanto   straordinario   gli   pareva   là
north wind   of the   all   so much   extraordinary   him   (it) seemed there
]   (of)

dentro   il   nome   di   galantuomo!
within   the   name   of   gentleman

In quella entrò una carovana di ladies e di lords,
In / that one / entered / a / caravan (crowd) / of / ladies (*English*) / and / of / lords (*English*)

colle sciarpe bianche nei capelli, cogli scarponi ferrati,
with the / scarves / white / in the / hats / with the / shoes / ironed (shod)

cogli alpenstok e riempirono tutto l'atrio.
with the / alpen walking sticks (*German*) / and / (they) filled up / all / the entrance hall

"Faccia el favorito piacere di non gridare. Quando non
Make / the (*dialect*) / special / pleasing / of / not / to yell / When / not

si sa viaggiare si sta a casa."
one / knows to travel / one / stays / at / home (should stay)

Questa osservazione piena di una saggezza antica fu
This / observation / full / of / a / wisdom / ancient / was

raddolcita da un "aspetti, abbia pazienza" più
softened / by / a / wait (wait please) / have / patience / more

amichevole, quasi fraterno, col quale il buon signore
friendly / nearly / brotherly / with the / which / the / good / gentleman

dava a vedere una prudenza non meno saggia e non
gave / to / see / a / caution / not / less / wise / and / not

meno antica.
less / ancient

Ma   la   notizia   che   un   "monsieur"   non   trovava   più   la
But   the   news   that   a   gentleman   not   found   (any)more the
                                        (*French*)

moglie,   messa   in   moto   dai   due   burloni,   aveva   già
wife   put   in   motion   by the   two   jokers   had   already

fatto   il   giro   di   mezzo   albergo,   dalla   cucina   alla   sala
made   the   turn   of   half   (the) hotel   from the   kitchen   to the   room

di   lettura.   Dietro   i   vetri   si   vedevano   dei   visini   pallidi
of   reading   Behind   the   glasses   one   saw   of the   faces   pales

e   gentili,   con   un   sorriso   anglo-sassone   sulle   labbra,   fra
and   kind   with   a   smile   anglo-saxon   on the   lips   between

la   pietà   e   la   canzonatura: da   un   andito   dietro   la
the   pity   and   the   scorn   from   a   little hallway   behind   the

scala   spuntò   per   un   istante   anche   la   tunica   bianca   di
stair   appeared   for   an   instant   also   the   skirt   white   of
(stairs)

"monsieur   le   chef" ,   un   cuoco   che   guadagnava   otto
Mr .   the   chef   a   cook   that   earned   eight
(*French*)

mila   lire   all'anno,   quante   sono,   o   quasi,   le   notti
thousand   lire   to the year   so many   (there) are   or   nearly   the   nights
                     (a year)

necessarie   per   fare   un   libro   che   nessuno   legge.
necessary   for   to make   a   book   that   nobody   reads

Uscì fuori finalmente anche il biondino, che condusse
Exited out finally also the little blond that lead
(little blond boy)

lo sposo per una seconda scala identica alla prima,
the spouse by a second stair identical to the first
(stairs)

ma collocata al di là d'un grazioso "jardin d'hiver" ; qui
but placed to the of there of a graceful garden of winter here
[at the other side] [winter garden , *French*]

stava l'imbroglio che il signor Malignoni non aveva
was the trick that the Mr . Malignoni not had

potuto districare.
been able to untie

L'aneddoto del "countryman" che in un "Hôtel d'Italy"
The anecdote of the countryman that in a Hotel of Italy
(*French*)

aveva perduta la sposa, fu stampato in molti magazzini
had lost the spouse was printed in many magazins

letterari con qualche variante, come si fa coi grandi
literary with some varying like itself makes with large
(it) (goes)

poemi epici.
poems epic

143   Due Sposi in Viaggio

The book you're now reading contains the paper or digital paper version of the powerful e-book application from Bermuda Word. Our software integrated e-books allow you to become fluent in Italian reading, fast and easy! Go to learn-to-read-foreign-languages.com, and get the App version of this e-book!

The standalone e-reader software contains the e-book text, and integrates **spaced repetition word practice** for **optimal language learning**. Choose your font type or size and read as you would with a regular e-reader. Stay immersed with **interlinear** or **immediate mouse-over pop-up translation** and click on difficult words to **add them to your wordlist**. The software knows which are low frequency and need more practice.

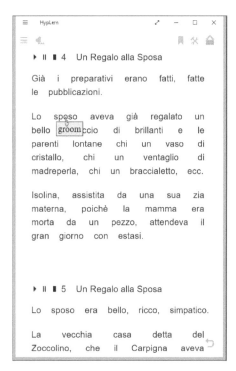

With the Bermuda Word e-book program you **memorize all words** fast and easy just by reading and efficient practice!

LEARN-TO-READ-FOREIGN-LANGUAGES.COM
Contact us using the button on the site!

Made in United States
Troutdale, OR
06/15/2023

10631863R00094